CRACK UP CRACK DOWN

The 33rd Ljubljana Biennial
of Graphic Arts

SLAVS AND TATARS

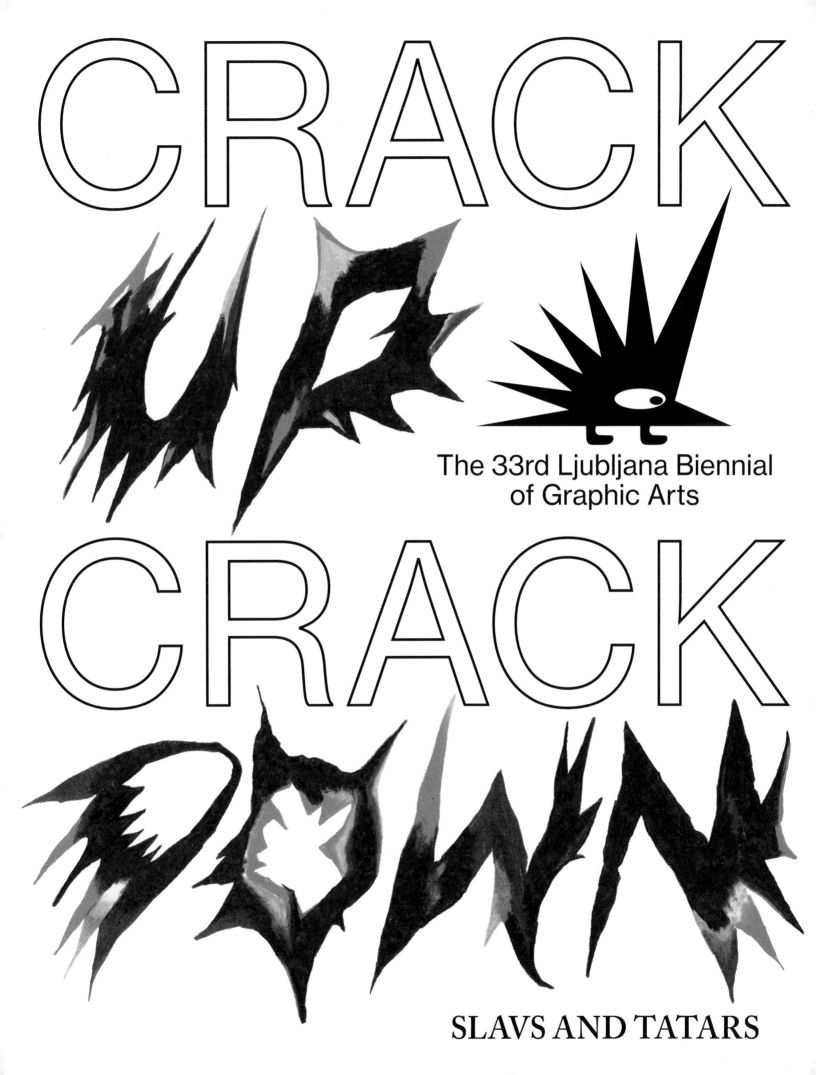

Lin May Saeed, ***Reiniger***, 2006.
Installation view at the 33rd Ljubljana Biennial of Graphic Arts, 2019.

TABLE OF CONTENTS

VISUAL ESSAYS

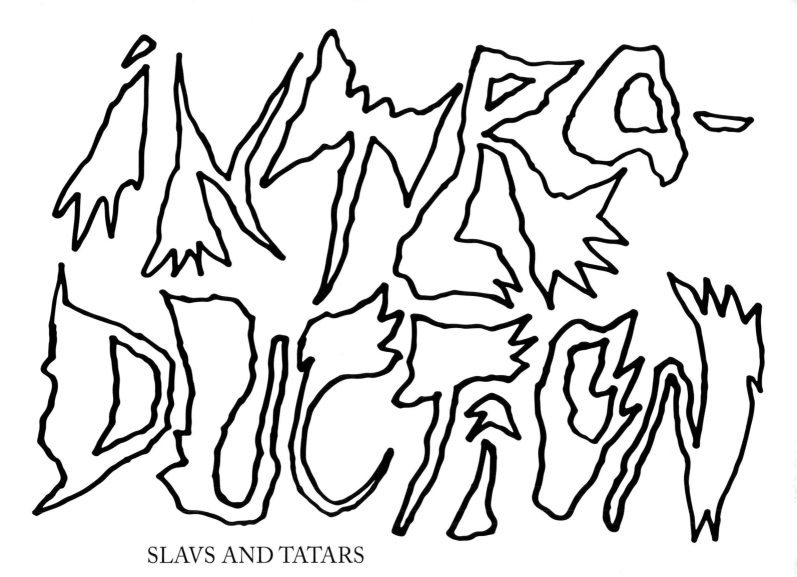

INTRO-DUCTION

SLAVS AND TATARS

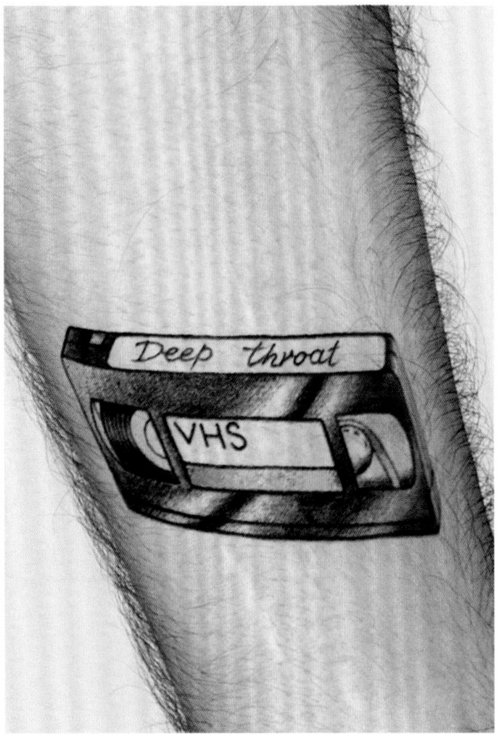

Homage to the **VHS cassette** by Studio Tatuażu Manta, Wrocław, Poland.

The graphic gets a bad rap. Some criticism is admittedly deserved. Some less so.

Contrary to popular perception, there is nothing millennial about the graphic arts. Their origins date to prehistory, when stencils of hands were made in caves in Asia, Europe, and the Americas some 35,000 to 40,000 years ago. It is the Industrial Era, though, that indulged the graphic arts as never before. The means of impressing text and image on various surfaces multiplied throughout the 20th-century, as did the facilities to do so. After all, the history of various artistic media is often tied to the economic exploitation of affiliated technologies; the pornography industry's use of VHS cassettes, for instance, made the relatively new technology increasingly accessible to emerging video artists in the 1970s.

What initially distinguished the ensemble of activities comprising the graphic arts – engraving, lithography, screen-printing, to name a few – from their more edified counterparts – painting and sculpture – was the ability to be reproduced, first by hand, then by machine. But a work of art draws its economic if not symbolic value from being unique and unavailable to all. Art trades on singularity and individuality, of both the creation and creator, too; the myth of the individual artist was born in the Renaissance, nurtured in the Romantic period, and greatly embellished in our

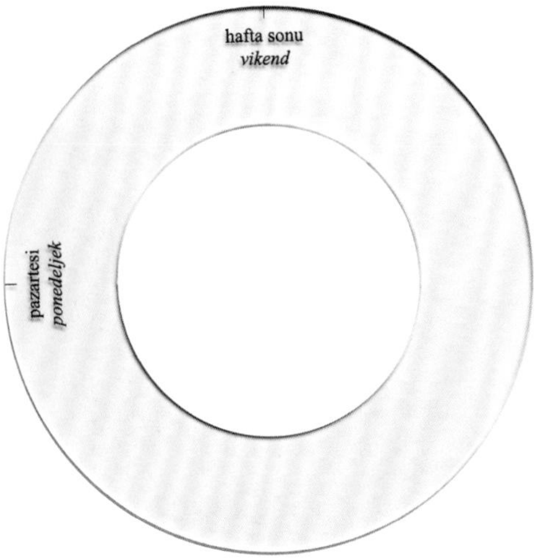

Cevdet Erek, ***Circular Week Ruler* (*Slovene edition*)**, 2019. From the Print Portfolio, The 33rd Ljubljana Biennial of Graphic Arts, 2019.

age of celebrity. The graphic arts tried to change this, to storm the Bastille of The One.[1] And like other revolutions, they made a good run of it. But ultimately failed.

The problem with revolutions, though, is not their failure or tendency towards filial cannibalism. If revolutions are fluid, as Zygmunt Baumann has written, the risk lies instead in their calcification. Today, in an age of increased automation, artificial intelligence, and Big Data, the graphic arts have become an *arrière-guard* stronghold of those obsessed with tactility. How ironic that a medium whose significance lay in its reproducibility clings desperately to outmoded notions of authorship and distinction.[2] As a joinder to the arts, the graphic has reversed course from its original *raison d'être*.

Slavs and Tatars embraced the phenomenal and phenomenological promiscuity of "the graphic" early in our practice. For the first three or four years, our work took place exclusively within the confines of print, be it the pamphlet, poster, or book. The affordability and reproducibility of print allowed us to share work directly with colleagues, friends, and the general public, bypassing the mediation of institutions, the crushing costs of art handlers, and not least the carbon footprint of crating.

It is this same auratic indiscretion which drew us to the Ljubljana Biennial of Graphic Arts. The Biennial's focus on graphic editions, prints, and other works on paper historically allowed for a democracy (with a small d) of access: print was relatively cheap,

***Rat* (*War*)**, a drawing by Robert, a 14-year-old refugee from Foča (Bosnia and Herzegovina, a former republic of Yugoslavia), 1993.

1.
Akin to an Abrahamic revolution in reverse, the graphic arts could have, would have, and should have returned a multiplicity to the reigning unicity and rarity of Art with a capital A. With increasing references to museums as the successors to cathedrals, as the temples of culture, it's only a matter of time before some will start writing A-t, as is done with G-d.

2.
Even more egregious than the fetishisation of the graphic arts is that of photography. The astronomical prices of certain photographer's books, the long lines of fans awaiting a signature of a new publication at Paris Photo, all must have Walter Benjamin turning in his unmarked Catalonian grave.

Miroslav Šutej, The 16th Ljubljana International Biennial of Graphic Arts, poster, 1985.

not only to make, more importantly, to send and share. That the graphic arts were championed by the Socialist Federal Republic of Yugoslavia was no coincidence: it was a resolutely internationalist medium of the mid-20th-century, one intimately associated with labour.

Now in its 33rd edition, the Ljubljana Biennial of Graphic Arts has a long and esteemed history. During the Cold War, Yugoslavia's non-aligned position made the exhibition one of the precious few meeting points possible between artists from the Warsaw Pact countries and those in NATO. Along with India and Egypt, Yugoslavia's leadership of the non-aligned movement articulated a crucial platform for anti-imperialist, anti-colonial, and anti-racist thought and action. But both the geopolitical importance and medium specificity of the Ljubljana Biennial came under attack in the late 1980s and early 1990s. The end of the Cold War and the subsequent Yugoslav Wars made a mockery of the country's non-aligned legacy, while conceptual art's increased viability, both institutionally and economically, did away with traditional understandings of artistic forms.

In an effort to re-engage with the heritage of the Biennial,

František Kupka, ***L'Assiette au Beurre***, magazine cover, 1902.

Stand-up comedy performance by Dragoş Cristian (pictured), Boštjan Gorenc - Pižama, Marina Orsag, Pavlo Voytovich, and Anja Wutej during the public programme of the 33rd Ljubljana Biennial of Graphic Arts, 2019.

3.
Mike Kelley had a particular fondness for artists as fools, which he contrasted with the curative role: "Beuys had a notion of art as a curative process. I don't have that delusion. Art doesn't cure you, it makes you aware of the problems you have. Art used to be a personal sickness that showed you were better than other people. In actuality art is just saying 'let's just point this out and we can talk about it, I'm no different from you, I'm no better than you, I'm not special, I'm no genius that cut off my ear. I'm just another schmuck like you.' What I like about Beuys is that he had a very egalitarian idea of art. I don't believe that either. A lot of people don't have the talent, the strength to stand outside the culture and make a fool of themselves. He was a professional fool. What I dislike about a lot of contemporary artists is that they want to be hipsters. They're not willing to be fools, to put themselves on the line in some shared emotional way. They want to be better than other people, and that's to me worse than wanting to be the outsider and tragic and a suicidal and all that crap."

4.
Anthony Gardner, "Curating Solidarity", paper presented at *Axis of Solidarity: Landmarks, Platforms, Futures*, 23–25 February 2019, Tate Modern, London, U.K.

we considered "the graphic" not as a medium *per se*, but rather as an agency. Such recourse imposes an editorial spine on an often supine formal exercise. For this edition of the Biennial, satire becomes the backbone. In particular, we asked: How does graphic language, designed for clarity or not, allow for the ambiguity crucial for art's affective potential, as well as its infra-political resistance? Slavs and Tatars have long held the view that critique, on its own, is a worthy if rather straightforward, stodgy, task. The frontal blow – sharp language, explicit message – leave us wanting. What is far more difficult is to pass a whack as a smack, a sock as a smooch. To deliver the critique with the airs of a festive grin, teeth gritted or not. Though each enjoys a distinct history, both the graphic arts and satire claim to speak for and to the people. With the rise of populism across the globe, in often reductive and revanchist forms, there has been a vigorous debate of late about who exactly constitutes "the people". For more than a millennium, satire has been a particularly effective, if contested, genre to explore this and other questions.

Often lauded for its ability to speak truth to power, satire has proven itself to be perhaps the original petri dish in a world of post-truth bacteria. A many-headed creature, satire has been considered by turns a form of popular philosophy, biting critique, or a conservative genre, given its moralising inclinations. It thrives in periods of authoritarian rule, from the rich tradition of communist humour in Central and Eastern Europe to the many examples from the Middle East. Today, the return of strongman rule in the West has witnessed a boom in comedy and satire.

Despite the dizzying turns of recent events, we would do well

Marionette of **Martin Krpan**, 1950. Made at the School of Applied Arts under the guidance of Božo and Ajša Pengov.

to follow the lead of our retroactive mascot, Hoja Nasreddin – the wise-fool often found riding backwards on his donkey – and look to the past to better understand the present.[3] The late 19th and early 20th centuries saw a proliferation of satirical journals across the globe: Germany's *Simplicissimus*, the United Kingdom's *Punch*, the Caucasus' *Molla Nasreddin*, France's *L'Assiette au Beurre*, or Slovenia's *Pavliha*, to name just a few. The affordability of print offered a tonic for those brutalised by the mechanisms of modernity, the Industrial Revolution in Europe and colonialism in the Middle East, Africa, and South Asia. It is no coincidence that the Ljubljana Biennial and the Bandung Conference of Asia-Africa débuted the same year, 1955.[4] Today, increased access to hardware and software, combined with social media platforms, provides a similarly fertile avenue for satire in renewed graphic forms, such as the meme or protest poster.

In the Biennial exhibition and in this volume, we invite the public to revisit the two historical G-spots of the Biennial, if you will: the geopolitical and the graphic. With a focus on our regional remit – in particular Eastern and South Eastern Europe – the contributors to this publication tell various stories about satire and question its relevance today. David Crowley examines episodes in 20th-century Eastern Europe where punk offered the passable ambiguity and encryption often associated with satire. Emily Apter offers a much-needed critical study of the meme as a form of micropolitics, mapping out its philological baggage and potential. Vid Simoniti underscores the equally subversive and conventional role of satire across specifically

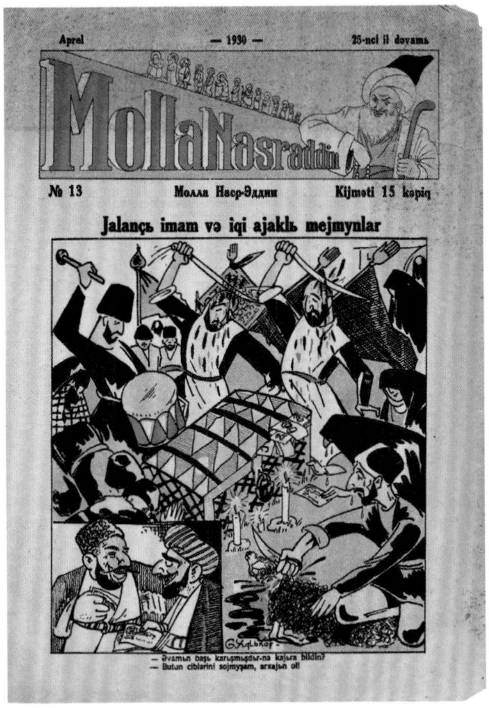

Molla Nasraddin, Vol. 25, No. 13, Baku, Azerbaijan, 1930. Founded by Jalil Mammadguluzadeh.

Pavliha, Vol. IV, No. 8, Ljubljana, 1947. Edited by Frane Milčinski, cover illustration by France Uršič, Slovene Association of Journalists.

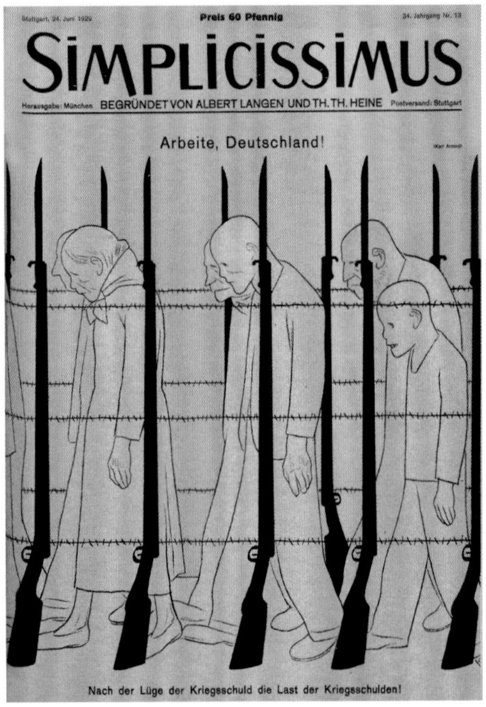

Simplicissimus, Vol. 34, No. 13, Munich, 1929. Magazine cover by Karl Arnold.

Slovenia's prime minister Marjan Šarec doing a double take, 2019.

Balkan examples, from the Slovenian archetypical folk hero Martin Krpan to the Bosnian TV sketch show *Top Lista Nadrealista*. Finally, M. Constantine explores the nexus of technology and affect which often accompanies satire, via the case of home videos shot in Sarajevo during the Balkan wars. Contributions by Metahaven, Mohammad Salemy, Goran Vojnović, Hamja Ahsan, Alenka Pirman with KULA, and Arthur Fournier and Raphael Koenig provide brief encounters with Alexander Vvedensky, introfadas, and Eduard Fuchs, amongst others.

Why satire? *Why not?* would be a good place to start. A former comedian is now Prime Minister of Slovenia, and another comedian is President of Ukraine. In recent years, many have noted with a mix of surprise and desperation, that reality is outstripping fiction. Those in Eastern Europe, if not the Global South, would argue that this is nothing new. As the famous Russian proverb goes, the future is certain, it's the past which is unpredictable.

Volodymyr Zelenskiy, President of Ukraine and comedian on the set of ***Servant of the People*** television series in Kyiv, Ukraine, 2019.

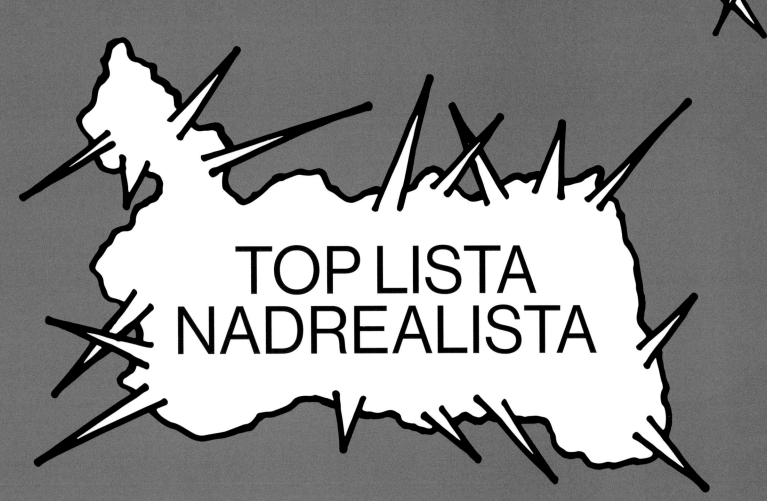

TOP LISTA NADREALISTA

A GLOSSARY OF TERMS

GORAN VOJNOVIĆ

The cult comedy show, *Top Lista Nadrealista* (*The Surrealists' Top Chart*), which originally ran from late 1984 to 1991, is one of the most ominous examples of satire foreshadowing reality in recent decades. Growing out of the New Primitivism movement, the show championed a local approach to conflict and language, even borrowing slang from Sarajevo *mahalas* (or "hoods"), and including many Turkish loanwords. Writer Goran Vojnović has compiled a glossary of terms and phrases that have influenced (and been influenced by) colloquial language throughout The Surrealists' Top Chart viewing public and beyond.

EPISODE: ***NJU PRIMITIVS***
(*NEW PRIMITIVES*)
THEME: RAT U FAMILIJI POPUŠLIĆ
(WAR IN THE SCREWEDINGTON FAMILY)

In the late 1980s, the conditions in Yugoslavia were perfect for satire. The country was invisibly disintegrating before the eyes of its inhabitants and this invisible disintegration created many visible cracks in the already fragile multi-ethnic society. It is almost impossible to distinguish between all the crises of that time: self-management socialism was in crisis, the Communist Party was in crisis, brotherhood and unity were in crisis, the country's economy was in crisis. Life in Yugoslavia was thus often on the verge of the absurd and one needed to distort reality only slightly to get to the grotesque. Thus, the New Primitivism art movement emerged, whose most prominent creation was the satirical TV series *Top Lista Nadrealista*.

Top Lista Nadrealista may have been conceived as a Balkan variant of *Monty Python's Flying Circus*, but its dark vision surpassed the British model. By mocking the socialist Absurdistan, the Surrealists created not only a lucid critique of society, but even more so, an ominous picture of the near future in which the grotesque would turn into a horror show. Even decades later, people would reproach themselves for not taking the Sarajevo jokers seriously.

The Yugoslavs laughed at a member of the Popušlići (Screwedington) family who, engaged in domestic warfare inside their apartment, victoriously shouts "*Zauzeli smo WC! Zauzeli smo WC!*" ("We took over the toilet! We took over the toilet!"), without realising that they were all Popušlići (Screwedingtons). Just like a boiling frog, the Yugoslavs spent the last years of their existence being cooked in black humour. The Surrealists' humour gradually grew blacker and blacker until people realised, albeit too late, that its blackness was merely the ashes of their former country.

SRANJE U RUANDI
(*SHIT IN RWANDA*)
NEMIRI U ŠVEDSKOJ
(UNREST IN SWEDEN)

In the *Nemiri u Švedskoj* (*Unrest in Sweden*) sketch, the Surrealists staged the Yugoslavs' relation to their own end with brutal precision. The Yugoslavs experienced the disintegration of their country so indifferently, as if it were something happening to the Swedes. The Eskimos wanted to secede, and penguins were the ones dying. We find an echo of this sketch in Tanović's *No Man's Land*, in the scene where a Bosnian soldier, reading a newspaper at the front, suddenly exclaims: "*Uuu, sranje u Ruandi!*" ("Look at this shit in Rwanda!")

In *The Guardian Weekly*, Aleksandar Brezar, a Bosnian journalist, tried to explain this scene by asking, "Might the unnamed soldier be so insensible to his own desperate situation, the death and destruction that defined the early days of Bosnia's independence, that the Rwandan genocide loomed larger in his mind?"

And if we paraphrase Brezar, we could ask: Were the Yugoslavs at the end of the 1980s so insensible to their own desperate situation, the death and destruction that defined the last days of Yugoslavia, that they were not capable of recognising themselves in the story about the Swedish refugees, the separatist Eskimos, and the dead penguins? Instead of recognising this, they said, "*Ma zdravo! Skrati priču! U Jugoslaviji problem! Zdravo!*" ("Good riddance! Cut the story short! Trouble in Yugoslavia! Good riddance!"). And then focused on the next news item.

MA ZDRAVO!
(*GOOD RIDDANCE!*)
ZGEMBO ADISLIĆ

Some years ago, a Croatian TV presenter tried in vain to persuade Branko Đurić to say "*Ma zdravo!*" ("Good riddance!") the way he said it while playing the role of Zgembo Adislić in the sketches of *Top Lista Nadrealista*. Đuro did not want to return to a world that had been long gone. Or he perhaps no longer wanted to speak the language of the Surrealists. The presenter stubbornly persisted, but Đuro, the most recognisable face of *Top Lista Nadrealista* other than Nele (Slobodan Janković, alias Dr. Nele Karajlić), did not want to go back. Or he could not. Perhaps he felt that it was improper to laugh at something that had turned out to be infinitely sad. (Whatever it was, I myself was very pleased he did not give in.)

Taking the Surrealists out of the temporal and spatial context in which they originated inevitably leads to the banalisation of their work, limiting it to superficial, even if first-rate, entertainment. The Surrealists are simply a composite part of the bloody end of Yugoslavia, which is why, even if it seems otherwise to us, they disappeared together with it. At some point, someone said to those times: "*Ma zdravo!*" ("Good riddance!") The end. Cut. Goodbye.

JA SAM IZ ESDEKA
(*I'M FROM THE IRS*)
NAGRADNA OTIMANJA
(PRIZE ABDUCTION)

"*Ja sam iz esdeka i ima sve da mi napismeno doneseš*" ("I'm from the IRS ... Make sure you have everything in writing"), is how Todor Zijan* threatens a TV journalist, while the crew is taking his television set out of

*
The name is no coincidence, as nothing with the Surrealists ever is, since *zijan* is a Turkish loanword meaning "damage, defect, or loss", while the character Todor or Kuku Todor is the wretched hero of a famous Serbian puppet show.

his apartment because he won the Prize Abduction game show.

This sentence reflects the Sisyphean resistance of the Yugoslavs against the unjust social system. But the absurd cannot be resisted, and Todor Zijan does not really resist the TV crew. He only gives them a piece of his mind. But to give someone a piece of one's mind is just another expression for the consolation prize of the losing team.

"*Svašta sam im nagovorio*" ("I told them all sorts"), repeated the Yugoslavs when they returned from the municipalities, *esdekajev* (the IRS), the post offices and the banks. That meant, "I didn't achieve anything, but I told them where to shove it." In the struggles with the system that were lost in advance, the Yugoslavs liked to have the final world. Or rather, the final curse.

HRKLJUŠ
(HRKLJUŠ)

Hrkljuš is a fictional sport created for television, says Wikipedia, originating in the imagination of the creators of *Top Lista Nadrealista*. *Hrkljuš* is a caricature of the Dervish ceremony in which the participants make a cut on their forehead with a knife, bandage it, and then start hitting it with the Quran to make the bleeding stronger. According to Wikipedia, the rules of *hrkljuš* are as follows: the players stand in a circle; the leader of the game throws a rag ball to someone in the circle; the players begin passing the ball to each other; whoever drops the ball leaves the circle, hitting themselves on the forehead with their fist and shouting, "*Do mene! Do mene!*" ("My bad!"). When the lead player shouts "*Hrkljuš!*", the player holding the ball is the winner. *Hrkljuš* is any player that has been eliminated. For them, the elimination is an act of humiliation, but the game continues until all players, with the exception of the winner, become *hrkljuši*.

Wikipedia also provides the meaning that the word *hrkljuš* took on once it passed from the sketch into lived language. If we are to believe it, *hrkljuš* means, among other things, "a stubborn persistence on a misguided path, and participation in a game whose rules are nebulous and changeable."

At its end, Yugoslavia thus became an ordinary *hrkljuš*. There was nothing else left for it to do but hit its forehead and shout: "*Do mene! Do mene!*" ("My bad!").

SELO VESELO
(JOYFUL VILLAGE)
SISANJE MOTKE
(SUCKING ON A STICK)

"*Jozo je katolik, ovaj je pravoslavan, ja sam musliman, ali mi to svi radimo jer je to prastari običaj koji svi poštujemo*" ("Jozo is Catholic, this one is Orthodox, and I am Muslim, but that's not important because we all do it, it's an ancient tradition that we respect"), explains Junuz Đipalo in the *selo Veselo* (Joyful Village), where people are still "enmoistened" and perform the collective *sisanje motke* (stick sucking). With a laugh, the New Primitives tell us that, underneath all the religions in Yugoslavia, primitivism still rules and connects its people.

However, the primitive and backward *sela Vesela* (Joyful Villages), which the Surrealists joyfully mocked, laughed last. The disintegration of Yugoslavia and the war that followed also led to the villages marching into the cities. The urban culture of New Primitivism disappeared overnight and left an emptiness that has not been filled yet. Thirty years after the end of Yugoslavia, many Yugoslav cities are merely big *sela Vesela* (Joyful Villages) ruled by trash and tradition. That is why, in the Balkans today, it is easier to imagine people, rather than new surrealists, sucking on a stick.

JA ČITAM
(I READ)
OTVORENO O JEZIKU
(OPENLY ABOUT LANGUAGE)

One of the Surrealists' most absurd prophecies – which actually came true – is precisely the one whose absurdity the people living in today's Croatia, Bosnia and Herzegovina, Serbia, and Montenegro do not want to acknowledge. If many find the existence of Eastern and Western Mostar absurd, most former Yugoslavs think that the carving up of the Serbo-Croatian language is quite logical. Croatian, Bosnian, Serbian, and Montenegrin are today four officially recognized languages, and only a handful of people pay heed to the linguists who claim that they are all one language with four linguistic standards.

The post-Yugoslav nationalistic politics hijacked language to the extent that, at a certain point, the Serbian films

- Hold it.
- Holding.
Sprejmi.
-Sprejeto.

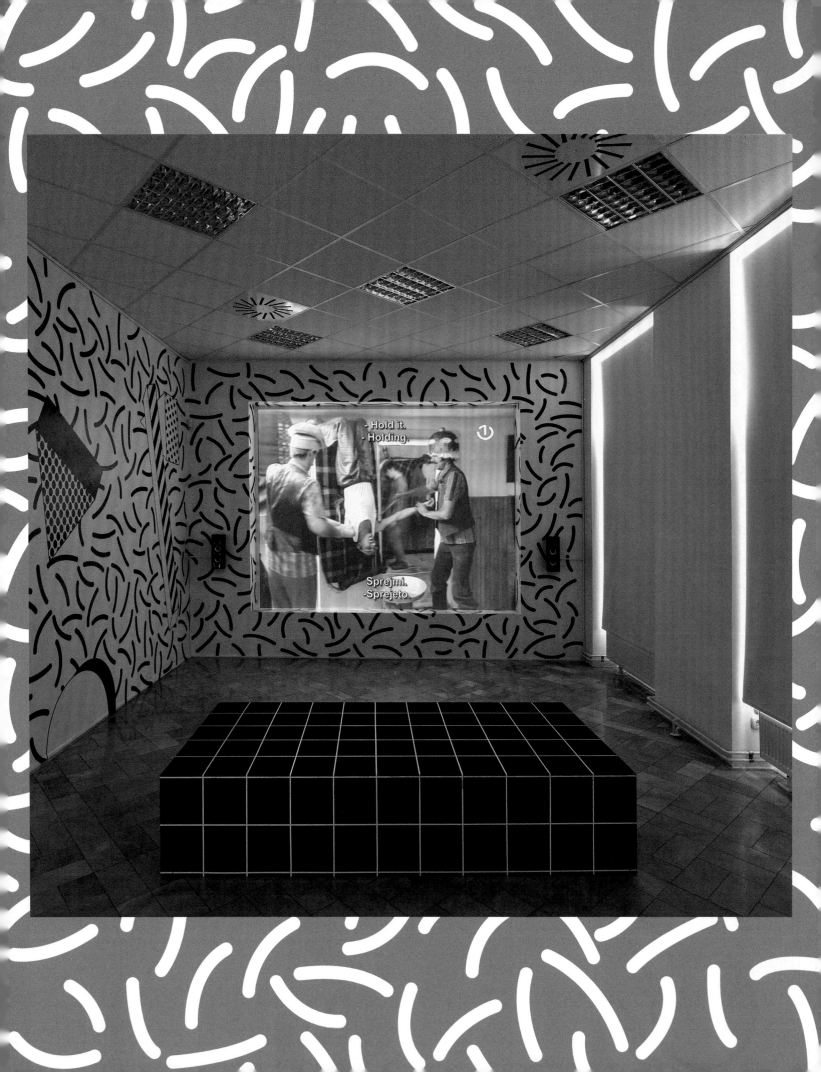

distributed in Croatia were subtitled: "*Jesen 1992*" ("The autumn of 1992") and written on the screen at the beginning of the film *The Wounds*, was also the subtitle "*Jesen 1992*" ("The autumn of 1992").

As someone who has been left without his mother tongue (the language of my parents, which used to be called Serbo-Croatian, no longer officially exists), I have no other choice but to occasionally take a look at the clip in which Dr. Nele Karajlić illustrates the obvious differences between Serbian and Croatian with the sentence "*Ja čitam*" ("I read").

ĐE BA ZAPELO?
(WHERE'S THE HOLD-UP?)
NOVA VALUTA
(NEW CURRENCY)

In the sketch, "*debazapelo?*" ("where's-the-hold-up?") is the name of one of the new currencies, and at the same time the unuttered question that accompanied the end of the 1980s and the time of the economic crisis. This question also brought forth the saviour in the shape of Ante Marković, a reformer who, according to one theory, just needed a bit more time and support from the people (who, at the fateful elections supported the nationalists, rather than Marković, despite the fact that numerous pop stars promoted him) to save Yugoslavia. The unbelievable inflation, restrictions on electricity and water, and the shortages of various products brought about by the crisis would later merge into a popular image of the former country, with which the post-communist anti-communists tried to prove to the post-Yugoslav Yugophiles how misconceived self-management socialism actually was. Their feeble-minded name-calling would in time displace the last remnants of the Yugoslavs' lucid self-irony.

"The average citizen of the Socialist Federal Republic of Yugoslavia earns a million dinars a month, but spends two," explains Tito to Khrushchev and Reagan in a very old joke. "How is that possible?" asks Reagan in amazement. Tito replies indifferently: "We're asking ourselves the same question."

Actually, the Yugoslavs asked "*De ba zapelo?*" ("Where's the hold-up?") with a similar indifference, since they saw it only as a rhetorical question. In Yugoslavia, there was always a hold-up somewhere. That is why people could not care less about whether Ante Marković really knew the answer to this question.

JEBENE NINĐE
(FUCKING NINJAS)
NINĐA REVIZORI
(NINJA AUDITORS)

In the *Ninđa revizori* (*Ninja Auditors*) sketch, a group of ninjas, whose black headgear reveals only their eyes, surround a student on a tram. They demand compliance with law and order and are not impressed by the student's knowledge. When they find out that he is riding the bus without a ticket, they beat him brutally. "*Pravda je ponovno zadovoljena*" ("Justice has been served once more"), one of the ninjas brags to the audience during the beating.

We cannot know how viewers at the time understood the sketch, but today's audience can certainly recognise in the ninjas Sarajevo's priests of various confessions, who, with their hypocritical concern for law and order, are turning a once (passably) multicultural, secular, and liberal country into a conservative bumfuck.

By the way, the Bosnians like to refer to various uniformed people, from Catholic nuns to women wearing burqas, as ninjas. *Jebene ninđe* ("Fucking ninjas"), they like to say. But it is unclear whether the credit for this should go to the Surrealists.

SARAJEVSKI ZID
(THE SARAJEVO WALL)
PODJELA SARAJEVA, SARAJEVSKI ZID
(THE DIVISION OF SARAJEVO,
THE SARAJEVO WALL)

The mythical line between the East and the West, which Orhan Pamuk claims is actually a line between the past and present – and which some people see in Istanbul, some in Sarajevo, and some on the Kolpa – had never been so clearly posited as by the Surrealists. The Sarajevo Wall became the most infamous symbol of their vision, as evidenced by the fact that there still exists something called *Istočno Sarajevo* (Eastern Sarajevo). But also, and above all, because it was precisely the Yugoslav War that showed how very distant the Yugoslav world had been from the West, and how big a wall there had been and

←
Top Lista Nadrealista, 1984–1991. Installation view at the 33rd Ljubljana Biennial of Graphic Arts, 2019.

still is on the border between Western and Eastern Europe.

And again, the end of the 1980s was a time of demolishing walls, a time when everyone laughed merrily at the surrealistic wall, but now, when walls are again being erected and the Balkans are ruled by visible and invisible barriers, the Sarajevo Wall is not in the least funny. This wall still stands and the majority of former Yugoslavs have remained on its sunless side.

ŠTRAJK MOZGA
(BRAIN ON STRIKE)
ŠTRAJK VLASTI
(THE GOVERNMENT ON STRIKE)

Although the tired, socialist Yugoslav society offered an easy target and receptive audience that had under communism gotten used to laughing at even the bitterest truths, this was still not enough for first-rate satire. If you do not believe me, think about the problems encountered by the comedians that try in vain to parody Donald Trump. Just like Yugoslavia, which often seemed like a first-rate parody of a state, Trump, for the most part, seems a first-rate parody of an American President, a parody that only the best comedians manage to exceed. Our impersonators of Slavoj Žižek have a similar problem: they still have not managed to create a funnier version than the man himself.

The fact that the Surrealists managed to parody the parody of a state so successfully is the best proof of their genius. And in parodying the parody, they nowhere went so far as in the sketch in which the government goes on strike and demands its rights – "*I mi bi da živimo ko rudari*" ("We would like to live like miners too") reads one of the banners. The government as a victim that we need to pity, sympathise with, and help: how familiar and how portentous this sounds today.

A BOGAMI I KEČIGA
(AND CERTAINLY STARLET)
ĐURINE KUĆNE ČAROLIJE
(ĐURO'S MAGICAL HOUSE TRICKS)

Branko Đurić Đuro is doubtlessly the most brilliant comedian among the Surrealists. Anything Đuro touched turned into a joke. He did not need satire. As a comedian, he is actually apolitical. *Đurine kućne čarolije* (*Đuro's Magical House Tricks*), a regular sketch of *Top Lista Nadrealista*, was actually a respite from politics and it is no wonder that *čarolije* (the tricks) were so popular and that Đuro became such a big star. Only a brilliant comedian can make "*A bogami i kečiga*" ("and certainly starlet") sound like the funniest phrase ever.

As opposed to most surrealistic sketches, *Đurine kućne čarolije* (*Đuro's Magical House Tricks*) is truly eternal. Even though it was made at the time of Oliver Mlakar and his "*jedna žličica Vegete*" ("one teaspoon of Vegeta"), to us today it seems like a parody of Jamie Oliver and the food-obsessed contemporary world.

Perhaps this is because, in the last forty years, while everything in the Yugoslav world has changed, only its cuisines have remained untouched; or perhaps because, under all the absurdity of disintegrating socialism, the Yugoslav reality was nevertheless not so different from today's.

Perhaps all states and all social systems are in their essence utterly absurd. Or perhaps today we just do not have any surrealists who could disclose all the absurdity of the world in which we live. Perhaps.

Bon appétit. Dober tek. Prijatno. Bujrum.

MARTIN KRPAN, TOP LISTA NADREALISTA, AND EQUALISING SATIRE

VID SIMONITI

Fran Levstik, Yugoslav stamp, 1965.

I meant to take my leave without a word. But since you have delayed my departure yourself, do not now be upset that I've told you a few harsh ones. You surely know what the late Jerry from the village of Golo used to say: 'Should I feed sweetmeats to the man I'm quarrelling with? Whichever spice stings him most, that's what I serve him!' And now good-bye, and stay in good health!
—Martin Krpan to the Emperor, in Fran Levstik's *Martin Krpan*[1]

I used to have a Swedish dentist. Like all dentists, he relished the pleasure peculiar to their profession – to converse with a person whom they have just rendered incapable of answering back. While thus engaged, this dentist also enjoyed the odd dig at my expense. He once told me of a journey through Yugoslavia, which he took as a younger man. He did not spare me sarcastic comments on the broken-down socialist trains, corrupt policemen, beautiful

1. Fran Levstik, *Martin Krpan z Vrha* (Ljubljana: Nova Založba, 1917), p. 27, translation V. S.

Tone Kralj, illustration for ***Martin Krpan z Vrha*** ("Krpan argues with the court"), watercolour, 1954.

women keen to marry a Westerner, etc. Of course I had to repay him somehow. So after I was finally allowed to spit out that abominable mixture of mouthwash and blood, I told him the following anecdote:

> *You describe my people rather well, I said, but, of course, we ex-Yugoslavs have also travelled to Sweden, mostly as immigrants, rather than as tourists. In fact, there was once a famous Yugoslav cigarette smuggler who emigrated to Sweden, and when he returned, everybody asked him what that country was like. 'Wonderful,' he said, 'in Sweden, public transport works flawlessly; people are kind and well-behaved; they have Abba; it is heaven on Earth. But there is one problem.'*

I waited for my dentist to raise an eyebrow.

> *'It is fucking boring.'*

What good can come from such low blows? This is the question of satire. Historically, satire has been a form of humiliation, propelled by humour and redeemed by self-righteousness. But in today's political climate – where old and new democracies alike are shaken by populist rebellions against consensus politics, by charismatic leaders that stoke xenophobic hatred, by Twitter wars unfolding between polarised factions – satire becomes an increasingly difficult subject. A few years ago, the coarseness of my conversation with the dentist left me feeling that a pleasing equality had been re-established between us. In today's fraught atmosphere, one is more wary of causing offense, and more suspecting of others' motives for causing it too. Perhaps, then, if a case is to be made for satirical modes of speech today, this is more easily done at some historical remove from the present.

* * *

Though I don't remember who the smuggler was in the anecdote I told the dentist, the story might have had some factual basis: Ratko Đokić, the boss of the Serbian cigarette mafia in Sweden, attained celebrity status in Belgrade, where he ran nightclubs and dated the pop singer Izolda Barudžija. But I begin this analysis of satire with another smuggler from my own corner of ex-Yugoslavia – the Slovenian national hero, Martin Krpan.

Fran Levstik's short story *Martin Krpan from Vrh* (1858) is a key part of the Slovene national literary canon. Krpan is an extraordinarily strong, good-natured man from the Slovene lands, who illegally trades in English salt. After a chance encounter with the Emperor, Krpan is called to Vienna, where he fights off a terrible giant, Brdavs, who is menacing the city. Published in the time of Bach's absolutism in the Austrian Empire, *Martin Krpan* is a satire of the Habsburg rule, disguised as a fairy tale. Levstik lampoons Viennese pretentions by juxtaposing them with Krpan's rural authenticity: the sophisticated dishes they serve Krpan at court are no match for his enormous appetite; he causes chaos by pulling imperial

Marlie Mul, ***Cigarette Hedgehog***, 2016.

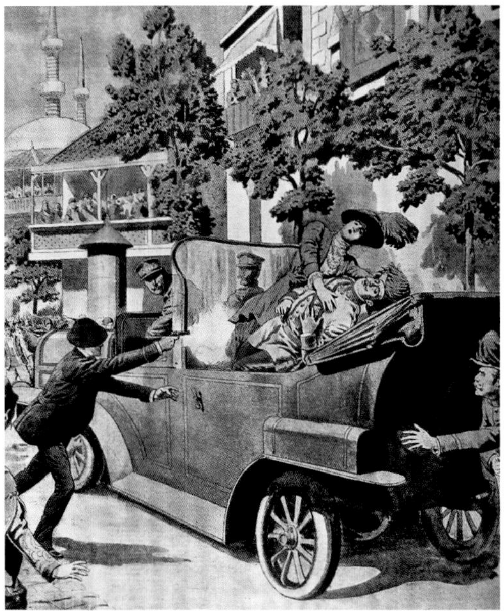

Achille Beltrame, ***Domenica del Corriere***, illustrating the assassination of Archduke Franz Ferdinand of Austria and his wife Sophie in Sarajevo on 28 June 1914.

Alina Bliumis, ***Nations Unleashed series: Barking Nations***, 2018.

Martin Krpan logo for sea salt, 2013.

horses out of the stables by their tails; he chops down an ornamental tree to make himself a club as a weapon. The Emperor himself is shown as kindly, but dithering and uxorious; the Minister of State, Gregor, is a boot-licking conniver.

In short, we have in *Martin Krpan* a classic example of dealing low blows to an opponent; or, to put it more precisely, an example of what Thomas Hobbes, in the 17th-century, described as the essence of humour: "The passion of laughter is nothing else but a sudden glory arising from a sudden conception of some eminency in ourselves, by comparison with the infirmity of others, or with our own formerly."[2] The sturdy Slovene suddenly, surprisingly triumphs over his German masters. Which is funny (to Slovenes).

While the idea of Krpan as a national hero has been the chief interpretation of the story, Krpan has had only mixed success in this regard since Slovenian independence. For some, Krpan's glory has not gone far enough: having defeated Brdavs, Krpan declines the honours that the Emperor would heap upon him and returns to his simple village life. In the 1990s, this seemed like slim pickings, and some scholars complained that Krpan's humbleness only confirmed the Slovenes' inferiority complex as citizens of a small, servile nation.[3]

For the liberal-cosmopolitan readers, on the other hand, Krpan gloats in his sudden glory rather too much. This pertains especially to his victory over Brdavs. Though Levstik never explicitly identified the giant with the Ottoman Turks, the context of an enemy besieging Vienna establishes him as such. The problem for the cosmopolitan reader, then, is that Krpan is an iteration of the "Christian frontiers" mythos. Slovenes' attempts at building a national identity, especially in literary works such as *Martin Krpan*, are here seen as predicated on the opposition to an Orientalised image of the Turkish Other. And, from today's (marginally) more tolerant standpoint, one might find such literature worryingly xenophobic.[4]

2.
Thomas Hobbes, *The Elements of Law Natural and Politic*, ed. F. Tönnies (London: Frank Cass & Co, 1969), p. 42.

3.
For an analysis of Krpan interpretations, see Bojan Baskar, "Ambivalent Dealings with an Imperial Past: The Habsburg Legacy and New Nationhood in ex-Yugoslavia", *Working Papers der Kommission für Sozialanthropologie Österreichische Akademie der Wissenschaften*. (2005), pp. 1–21, here 8–10.

4.
See the analysis in Alenka Bartulović, "'We have an old debt with the Turk and it best be settled': Ottoman incursions through the discursive optics of Slovenian historiography and literature and their applicability in the twenty-first century", in Božidar Jezernik, ed., *Imagining 'the Turk'* (Newcastle-upon-Tyne: Cambridge Scholars Publishing, 2010), pp. 111–136.

Hinko Smrekar, ***Self Portrait***, 1926.

And so Krpan can hardly satisfy anyone today: he is not quite the nation-building hero, and is even less of a committed multiculturalist. But neither of these complaints quite get the right end of *Martin Krpan*, nor do they capture what is the most curious aspect of this story *as a satire*. What a satire can do, certainly, is deliver a bout of "sudden glory", i.e., humiliate the opponent and elevate the protagonist. But it can also satirise *the protagonist*.

The idea of Krpan as a national hero is so well-ingrained in the Slovene literary psyche, that the suggestion that his character is itself the subject of satire may sound like an open heresy. However, it is striking what an uncouth, oddball rustic Levstik portrays him to be. No doubt Krpan is strong and cunning, but he is also ill-mannered and quick to anger. His speeches in Vienna are full of obscure references to village life, which must strike his interlocutors as bordering on insane ramblings. See the epigraph to this essay, for example. Here, having fallen out with the Empress, Krpan is about to leave the court in a huff; in a lengthy tirade, he tells the Emperor he must 'surely know' what Jerry (Jernejko) from Golo, a small village near Ljubljana, had to say on such occasions.

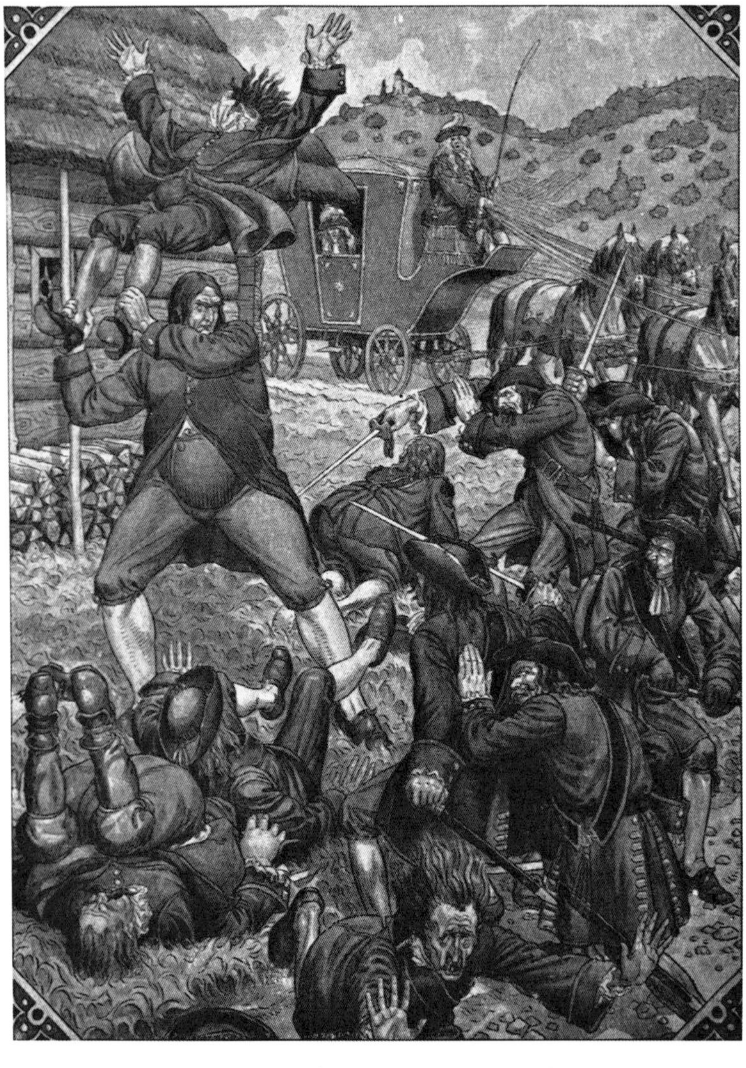

Hinko Smrekar, illustration for ***Martin Krpan z Vrha*** ("Krpan beats the toll officers"), ink drawing, 1917.

Hinko Smrekar, illustration for ***Martin Krpan z Vrha*** ("Krpan wrecks the armoury"), ink drawing, 1917.

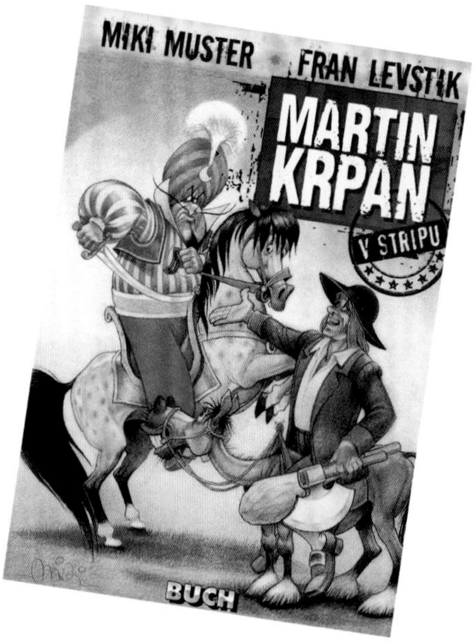

Miki Muster, ***Martin Krpan v stripu***, 2018.

Who the hell, might the Emperor rightly ask here, is Jerry from Golo? When the Emperor offers Krpan the Princess' hand in marriage, Krpan's rejection is also quite strange (queer, even). He decidedly prefers his widowhood, and his long-winded account of his first marriage implies that his wife's death came as something of a relief. Of course, Krpan *is* the protagonist of the story, but might we not also see in him the image of an eccentric village bachelor, rather than a paragon of nation-building virility?

Among the visual renditions, however, only Hinko Smrekar's illustrations of 1917 capture Krpan's parodic character. Unlike in Tone Kralj's sumptuous watercolour illustrations or Miki Muster's comic book, which both show a youthful and strapping Krpan, Smrekar shows Krpan as a middle-aged man, wider at the waist than at the shoulders. When he fights off the toll collectors, his heavy stomach hangs out in front of him. Wrecking the imperial armoury, he stares at the Emperor in dim-witted frustration, as if expressing a big fat "oops". Riding his trusty mare, his feet are almost dragging on the ground.

While the giant Brdavs is in all visual renditions an unmistakable heir of the early modern *imago Turci* – images of turbaned, cruel invaders that proliferated in European visual culture of the early modern period – we might recognise in Levstik's and Smrekar's Krpan an echo of the 'lewd peasant' stereotype, an echo of what we might call *imago rustici*. Consider *Martin Krpan* next to, say, 16th-century satirical prints of peasant life, such as this 1527 German woodcut of a peasant wedding: burly peasants consume inordinate amounts of food, while one of them (at the bottom-right corner of the table) vomits and another (at the bottom-left) defecates. Such images deriding peasants as lewd, voracious, and sexually perverse were common from the early modern era well into the 19th-century; and, as Umberto Eco notes in his study *On Ugliness*, such prints and literature tended to laugh *at* the peasants, rather than *with* them.[5] Krpan, of course, possesses many redeeming features, but doesn't he also share these peasants' rude appetites? At court he consumes, as Levstik puts it, "two legs of pork, two quarters of a ram, three capons, and, since he would not eat the middle, the crust of four white loaves of bread, smeared with eggs and butter."[6] Does he not share their cunning, coarseness, and even perhaps their strange sexual proclivities? In spite of any admiration Krpan may win, these elements also call forth an almost contemptuous smile.

Erhard um Schön, ***Peasant Wedding***, woodcut, 1527.

If we accept that the protagonist's character in *Martin Krpan* is also itself the target of satire, this suggests a rather surprising literary structure, one that is at odds with traditional views of the genre. Throughout its long history, satire has encompassed many varieties and subcategories – including the Roman genres practised by Horace and Juvenal, or the grotesque Renaissance satire of Rabelais – but the modern European conception of satire can perhaps be traced to the 17th and 18th centuries, to the work of such satirists as Jonathan Swift, John Dryden, or Voltaire.[7] These authors share the view that satire is partial to a given social, religious, or moral position; in John Dryden's formulation, the satirist is obliged "to give his Reader some one Precept of Moral Virtue; and to caution him against some one particular Vice or Folly."[8] In this same vein, *Martin Krpan* has often been understood as a satirical attack on (the vices and

5. Umberto Eco, *On Ugliness* (London: MacLehose Press, 2011), p. 137.

6. Levstik, *Martin Krpan*, p. 13, translation V. S.

7. Dustin Griffin, *Satire: A Critical Introduction* (Lexington: University Press of Kentucky, 1994).

8. Cited in Dustin Griffin, "Dryden and Restoration Satire", in Ruben Quintero, ed., *A Companion to Satire* (London: Blackwell, 2007), p. 177.

follies of) the Habsburg multinational state. However, insofar as we can also see the character of Krpan himself derided, this rather complicates matters. Here, not only Levstik's *counter-position* (Austrian rule) but also his own position (Slovene authenticity) receives satirical treatment. In *Martin Krpan*, there is a strange equality between the three equally-made-fun-of opponents: the bungling Emperor, the bloodthirsty Turk, and the Slovene country bumpkin.

Kikeriki (Vienna, 20 October 1918). A cartoon in the Austrian newspaper depicting the children of Lady Austria leaving her behind. Only the German child stays with her.

Quentin Massys, ***Ill-Matched Lovers***, oil on panel, ca. 1520–1525.

I shall leave aside the question as to what extent Levstik himself consciously intended to satirise the character of Krpan; the satirical potential is made palpable enough by Smrekar's illustrations. The key question is whether a model of satire revealed – an *equalising satire*, which attempts to humiliate *all* the political positions on the table – can play a productive role at the intersection of art and politics today. Before I attempt a more theoretical unpacking of this notion, let me introduce another instance of such equalising satire.

* * *

The wartime episodes of the comedy television show *Top Lista Nadrealista* (1993), filmed during the siege of Sarajevo, must surely be a case of satirical humour produced under the most extreme circumstances in recent history. *Top Lista Nadrealista* (*The Surrealists' Top Chart*) originally grew out of the New Primitivism music movement in Sarajevo in the late 1980s, and soon came to enjoy a Yugoslavia-wide popularity.[9] The show's creators – the most recognizable onscreen presences were Nele Karajlić, Branko Đurić, and Zenit Đozić – initially modelled themselves on Monty Python, producing absurdist,

9. For some sources in English, see: William Hunt, Ferida Duraković, Zvonimir Radeljković, "Bosnia Today: Despair, Hope, and History", *Dissent* 60.3 (2013), pp. 23–26; Borislava Vučković, "Dr. Nele Karajlić in the Framework of the 'New Primitives'", *Muzikologija* 23 (2017), pp. 99–115.

Tala Madani, ***Dirty Protest***, 2015.

The cast of ***Top Lista Nadrealista***, 1984–1991.

Illustration from the exhibition ***Yugoslavia: From Beginning to End***, Museum of the History of Yugoslavia, 2012–2013.

and mostly politically harmless sketches, interspersed with musical interludes. However, the final two seasons of the show (1989 and 1991) presented openly political material that was darkly prophetic of the calamity about to happen. One sketch imagined a Sarajevo divided between warring garbage collectors; another showed a divorced couple at war in a divided apartment.

As the war broke out and Sarajevo came under siege in 1992, production ceased and several of the makers of *Top Lista Nadrealista* left the city (Branko Đurić, for example, escaped to Ljubljana, where he launched a renaissance in Slovenian comedy). Those who stayed behind assembled a new group, continued with the radio show, and even produced a few television episodes. With both Karajlić and Đurić gone, these wartime episodes were a spin-off of the original series, and they are certainly not as well-known today as the sketches of 1989 and 1991, but they do stand as a remarkable document of satire in wartime.

The portrayal of different ethnicities in wartime *Top Lista Nadrealista* is of special interest here: the tenor of the entire show is anti-war, and yet, the sketches often base their comedy on satirical ethnic stereotypes.[10] To a harsh critic this might appear to be a paradoxical or even hypocritical position. After all, ethnic jokes – as Simon Critchley has noted in his book *On Humor* – always express contempt of the ethnically Other.[11] Eliciting Hobbesian "sudden glory", such jokes seem to reinforce hierarchies of ethnic value, of the sort necessary to undertake nationalist wars. But the wartime *Top Lista Nadrealista* pushes us towards a more complex understanding of such humour.

In one sketch, a Roma (Gypsy) man is digging a tunnel into the ground to escape the war. He declares that he has had "enough of democracy".[12] His wife (a male actor in drag) and his children (who seem to be genuine Roma children co-opted into the sketch) bemoan the man's attempt to leave, but the punchline

10. These stereotypes are often based on "nesting Orientalisms", whereby each ethnicity is differentiated from the others in terms of how "Oriental" or "Balkan" it is. Milica Bakić-Hayden, "Nesting Orientalisms: The case of former Yugoslavia", *Slavic Review* 54.4 (1995), pp. 917–931.

11. Simon Critchley, *On Humour* (London: Routledge, 2002), pp. 68–76.

12. *Top Lista Nadrealista 4*. Co-production of Radio-Televizija Bosne i Hercegovine i Top Lista Nadrealista, Sarajevo, 1993–1994. Viewed at https://www.youtube.com/watch?v=XMNMb8t9Lsk&t=564s. Accessed 19 December 2018.

comes when the man tells us he is planning to dig the tunnel through the Earth's core. In the ensuing scenes he pops up in various parts of the warzone, where he is threatened by everybody from the Russians to UN troops, before digging his way back home. Another sketch stages a report by an "enemy" TV station from Serbia. The Serbian forces have caught two Czech tourists, who they suspect of being Mujahedin fighters aiding the Muslim Bosnians. Much of the humour derives from a silly confusion between the words "tourist" and "terrorist", and other misunderstandings between the two Slavic languages.

Stills from ***Top Lista Nadrealista*** at the 33rd Ljubljana Biennial of Graphic Arts, 2019.

The set-up in these sketches relies on the stock characters from the "Balkan jokes", a near-endless catalogue of ethnic witticisms familiar to all denizens of the former Yugoslavia. The Roma are shown as a happy-go-lucky group. They all burst into song in the end; the children are shown with stereotypical Roma moustaches; the husband is briefly shown stealing a car battery. The Serbian reporter has bushy facial hair associated with Serbian Orthodoxy; the Czech tourists have the childlike manners and unfashionable clothes which they always had in the Yugoslav imaginary. Even today, the word "Czech" remains a Slovenian colloquialism for "outmoded", stemming from the time when Czechoslovakia had less access to Western fashions than Yugoslavia.

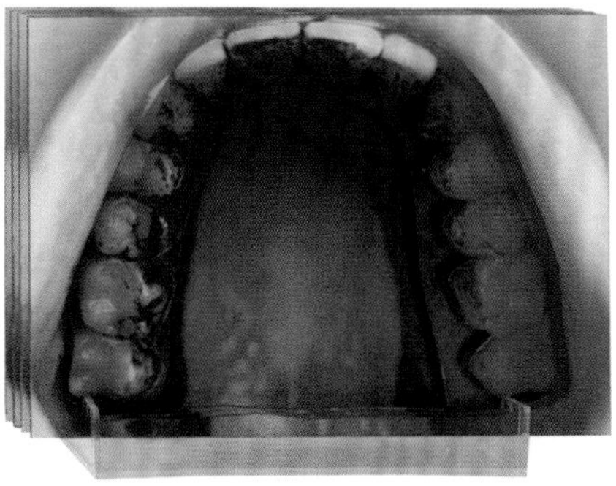

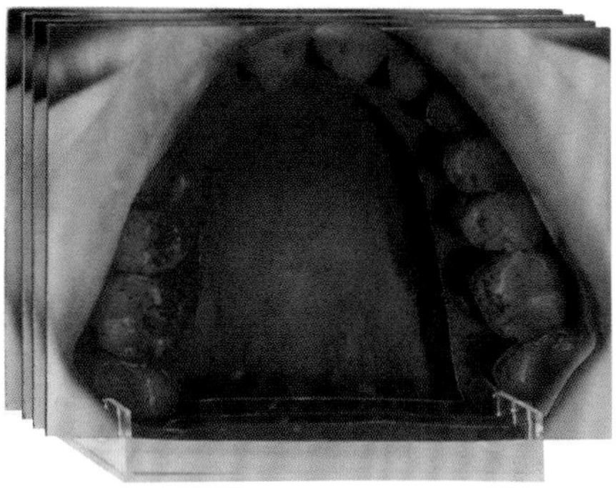

To say that these sketches – like most Balkan jokes – employ crude ethnic stereotypes would be entirely correct. It would also be right to say that the sketches, produced in the Bosnian-controlled territory, tended to be told from the perspective of Muslim Bosnians. But these wartime sketches are also self-deprecating to the point of fatalism: showing, for example, a Bosnian commander who accidentally gives away the co-ordinates of his headquarters and ends up getting bombed as a result.[13] By employing stereotypes, the Sarajevo Surrealists keep the animosities of war in view, and yet the effect is not one of jingoist self-aggrandisement. What comes across instead is the sense that all these stock characters from the old, familiar Balkan jokes are trapped in the horror and absurdity of war together.

Despite the century-and-a-half time lapse between them, what *Top Lista Nadrealista* and *Martin Krpan* share is the "equalising" element in satire. In both cases, mutually opposing political agents are brought into view, and are shown to be humorously, but *equally*, deficient. Hobbes' idea of humour as "sudden glory" does not quite work here, because in this case a sudden infirmity, or sudden humiliation, applies to all involved. The ideals have tumbled and all that remains to be seen is the grotesque struggle in which human bodies are now entangled.

* * *

'NAƱ OR 'NƏƱ

"Now Jump!" were the last words a Dutch tourist heard as she leaped off a bridge in Cabezon de la Sal in Northern Spain in 2015. From those words she had, all too quickly, deduced that her bungee rope was secured and ready to spring her back from her downward flight. It was not. The bungee jump instructor was arrested and before a trial he explained that he had not said "Now Jump!" but rather "No Jump!", meaning that his thick Cantabrian accent when speaking the English letter "o" had led to the fatal misunderstanding. Despite only pleading guilty to a poor command of English, he was convicted of manslaughter and sentenced to four years in prison.

Lawrence Abu Hamdan, ***Disputed Utterances (dioramas)***, 2019.

Satire may seem cynical. The free reign of oppressive stereotypes in satire appears unconscionable and cruel at a time of crisis. If we accept the "equalising" element to satire, then one might also be disappointed that satire does not take sides more clearly, and instead reduces all positions – the "good" and the "bad" – to the same mud-slinging level. To return to my micro-political situation in the dentist's office, would it not have been better to rise above petty divisions, to be the better man, to say a word that would inspire tolerance or kindness? Of course, I would like to say "no" here. But it is not theoretically straightforward to show why satire is not cynical, how its subversion of ideals can be politically productive.

To resist the conflation of satire with cynicism, we might begin with a thought by Slavoj Žižek (admittedly written in a different context) in an essay on the European refugee crisis: "Communitarianism is not enough: a recognition that we are all, each in our own way, strange lunatics provides the only hope for a tolerable co-existence of different ways of life."[14] Equalising satire may offer a step towards such a realisation. Consider, again, the Czech tourists sketch in *Top Lista Nadrealista*. The Czechs keep repeating they are Czechs, the Serbian journalist spouts patriotic platitudes, and the entire segment is framed by a (presumably Bosnian) text crawler suggesting it is "footage taken from the aggressor's television." But the more the seriousness of national divisions is emphasised by all concerned, the more absurd they appear, especially given the obviously ill-fitting fake beard of the "Serbian" journalist and the farcically hysterical "Czechs". We would misunderstand the sketch if we saw it as simply mocking different peoples; it is instead the idea of belonging to any national category that begins to look like lunacy.

13. *Ibid.*

14. Slavoj Žižek, "Terrorists with a Human Face", in Jela Krečič, ed., *The Final Countdown: Europe, Refugees and the Left* (Ljubljana: IRWIN, 2017), pp. 187–201, here 199.

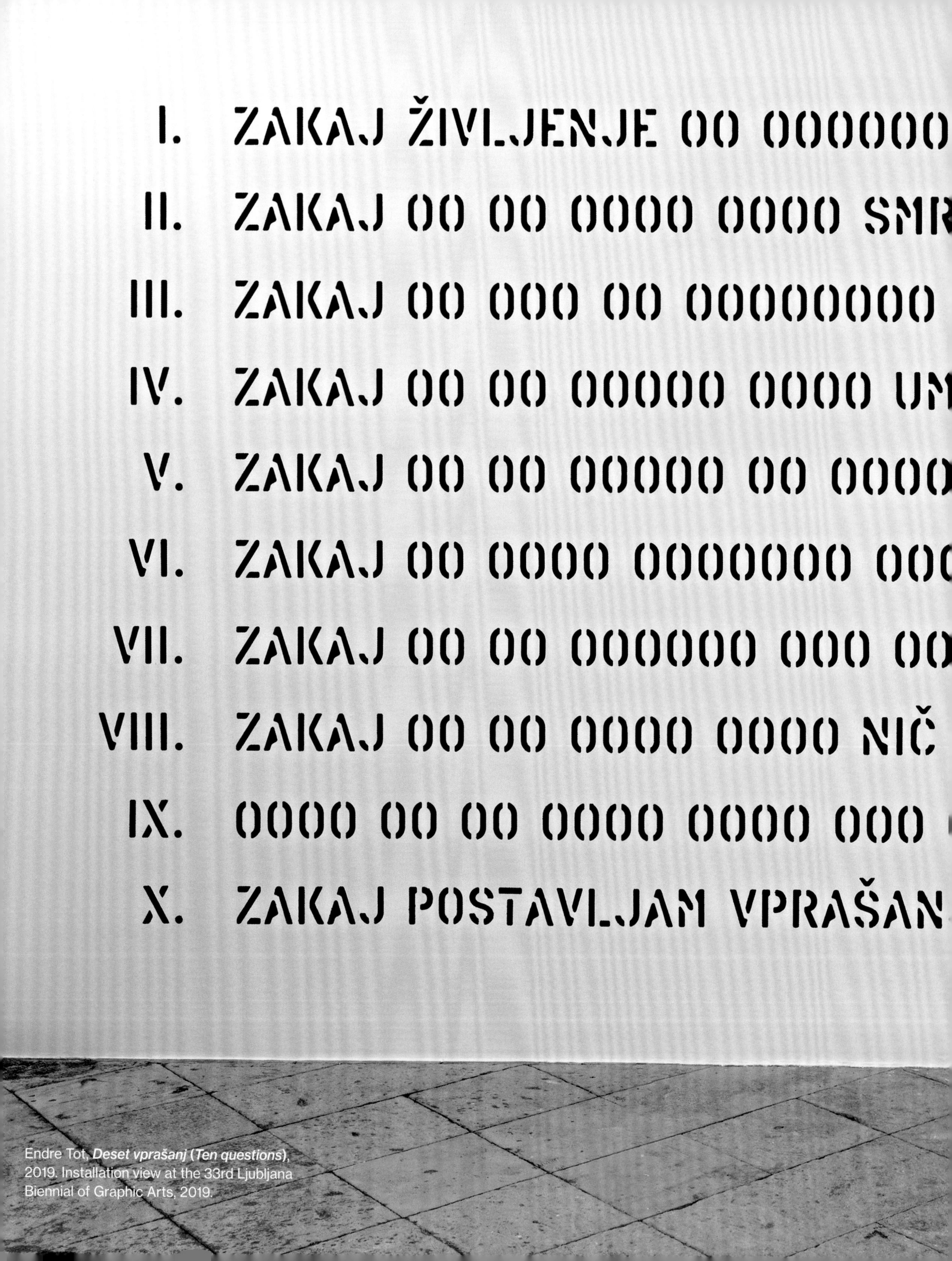

Endre Tot, ***Deset vprašanj*** (***Ten questions***), 2019. Installation view at the 33rd Ljubljana Biennial of Graphic Arts, 2019.

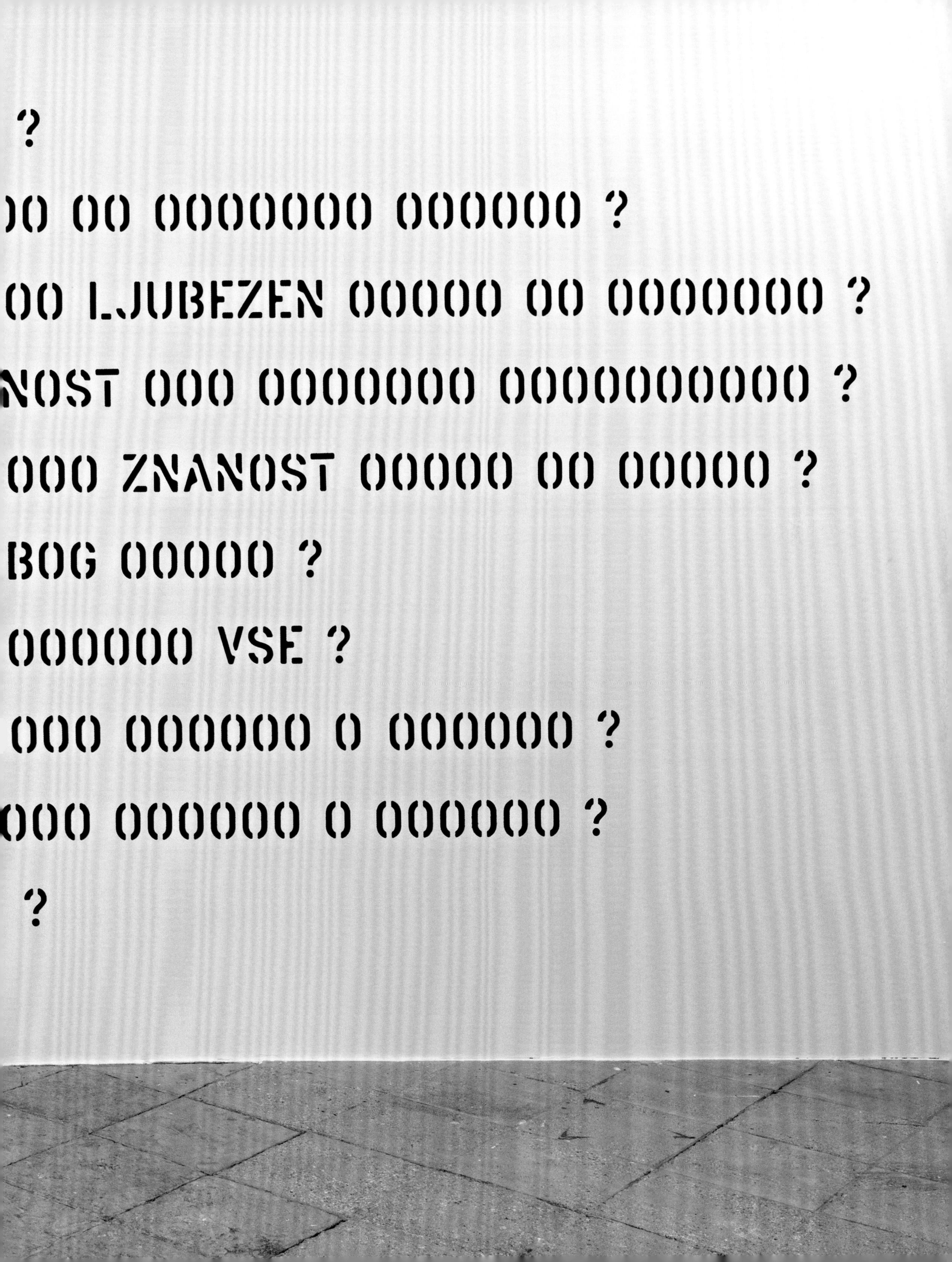
?
00 00 0000000 000000 ?
00 LJUBEZEN 00000 00 0000000 ?
NOST 000 0000000 0000000000 ?
000 ZNANOST 00000 00 00000 ?
BOG 00000 ?
000000 VSE ?
000 000000 0 000000 ?
000 000000 0 000000 ?
?

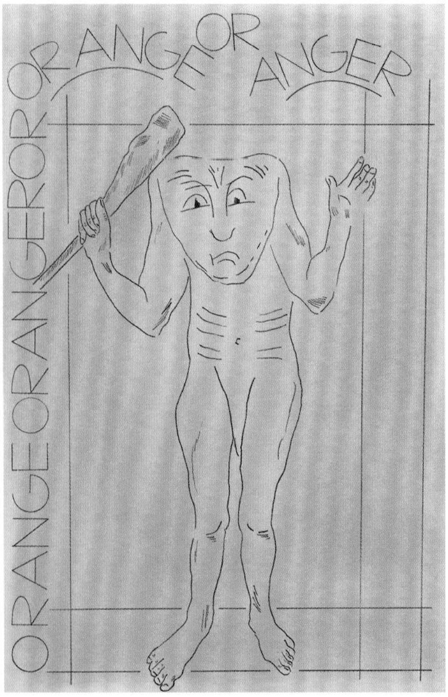

Honza Zamojski, ***Mindless Anger***, 2019.

We may further illuminate the mechanism at work here by borrowing from Alenka Zupančič's theory of comedy. Zupančič distinguishes between "false" comedy – which merely tarnishes some ideal type with vulgarity – and "true" comedy – which subverts the ideal type itself. In conservative comedies of baronage, for example, aristocrats are shown to chase after women, fart, and snore: they are shown as "merely human", but the aristocratic order itself is not questioned. "True" comedies, by contrast, show an aristocrat as silly in the very belief that he is an aristocrat; here Zupančič builds on Jacques Lacan's remark that "a lunatic is a king who believes that he really is a king."[15] Perhaps this is the politically productive moment in equalising satire too; in various sketches of *Top Lista Nadrealista*, (ethnic) ideals are dismantled precisely through such excessive affirmation.[16] The best-known example of this is the pre-war "languages" sketch, which mocks the nationalist attempts to recognise Croatian, Bosnian, and Serbian as separate languages, when in reality these are mutually intelligible. What makes the sketch so funny is that all the characters play along faithfully with the ideal, and are completely uncomprehending of each other, until another person's language (Bosnian) is translated into their own (Serbian). What is said, of course, sounds exactly the same. By undermining multiple positions, equalising satire subverts some overarching "bad" ideal – say, nationalism, as such.

Yet this only partially addresses the trouble with satire. Where satire differs from the "subversive" model of political art (postulated by Zupančič's view of comedy, but of course also espoused in poststructuralist aesthetics more broadly), is that satire does not in fact replace one set of ideals (say, nationalism) with another (say, cosmopolitanism). Indeed, while satire may mock any number of ideals, it *leaves them in place* insofar as it fully utilises their oppressive aspects; the taxonomies, the stereotypes, the "otherings" that they produce. For example, while *Martin Krpan* and *Top Lista Nadrealista* both expose the absurdity of their respective political and symbolic orders, they also never abjure the stereotypes, Orientalisms and divisions which were enshrined in those very orders. In the illustrations for *Martin Krpan*, Turks are still murderous and have long moustaches; in wartime *Top Lista Nadrealista*, Serbs are still bloodthirsty and have bushy eyebrows.

This troublesome aspect of satire may be perhaps more fully appreciated if we consider examples closer to us in time: the excessive, neo-Rabelaisian Anglophone satires of the 2000s, such as those of Sacha Baron Cohen (*Borat*, 2006; *Bruno*, 2009), or of Trey Parker and Matt Stone (*South Park*, since 1997; *Team America*, 2004). These share something of the equalising structure I described: they not only mock ideals that cosmopolitan-liberal audiences perceive as "bad" (various domestic and imperialist forms of American chauvinism), but also those they perceive as "good" (environmentalism, sexual tolerance, multiculturalism). In the process, such satires mercilessly unleash all kinds of oppressive categories: stereotypes of Islamic terrorists, Third World immigrants, homosexuals, rednecks, and so forth. For example, while Sacha Baron Cohen's *Borat* might make conservative American ideals its main target, it also punches down, and punches hard, at the figure of the Third World

15.
Alenka Zupančič, *The Odd One In: On Comedy* (Cambridge, MA: The MIT Press, 2008), pp. 30–37.

16.
Comparable strategies may be detected in Soviet "stiob" humour as well, as well as in what Slavoj Žižek described as over-identification in the Slovene punk band Laibach. See e.g. Dominic Boyer and Alexei Yurchak, "American Stiob: Or, What Late-Socialist Aesthetics of Parody Reveal About Contemporary Political Culture in the West", *Cultural Anthropology* 25.2 (2010), pp. 179–221.

Still from ***South Park***, season 20, 2016.

immigrant. If we were to suggest simply that *Borat* "subverts" xenophobia by over-affirmation, we would not be telling the full story. The satirist leaves the stereotypes of the old order lying around, like so many weapons for its audiences to use.

Such trouble may be inherent to satire. But what *Top Lista Nadrealista* and *Martin Krpan* teach us is that the best satirical positions do not temper their use of oppressive categories with a final "just kidding." Rather, they are those that allow us to see the violence of such categories most clearly. In wartime *Top Lista Nadrealista*, of course, the threat of violence is always literally present, filmed as it was during the siege of Sarajevo. But even *Martin Krpan*, while often presented as a children's story, has violence at its core: Brdavs murders the Emperor's son, and Krpan decapitates Brdavs. Of the various illustrators, Smrekar again stands out for capturing this violent aspect. Towering over the unlucky prince, Smrekar's Brdavs is a gaunt, skeletal figure, his mouth grimacing in a deathly grin. Krpan's confrontation with the toll collectors – a colourful dance in Tone Kralj's beautiful illustration – is the work of a scowling, maddened hulk in Smrekar's rendition. While in the illustrations of Tone Kralj and Miki Muster, the two combatants appear to be playfighting in a jocular historical re-enactment. Smrekar's warring giants promise destruction. In other words, while equalising satire indeed shows that we are *all* lunatics, its position need not be the false hope that we can all just get along, or the cynical assertion that no one position is better than another.

Hinko Smrekar, illustration of Brdavs for ***Martin Krpan z Vrha*** ("But the giant was not of a merciful heart, but murdered every opponent that he would beat in combat"), ink drawing, 1917.

Still from ***Team America: World Police***, 2004.

To elaborate on the value of such satirical ruthlessness for political discourse, we might inscribe satire within a realist tradition of political philosophy, the tradition of Machiavelli, Hobbes, Carl Schmitt, or more recently, of Chantal Mouffe's approach to politics as an agonistic struggle between adversaries.

Tone Kralj, illustration for ***Martin Krpan z Vrha*** ("Krpan fights the toll collectors"), watercolour, 1954.

Borrowing a term from Mouffe, we might say that satire reveals politics as a form of "agonistic pluralism".[17] For Mouffe, "the political" consists in a confrontation between interests that cannot be aligned. The task of politics, then, is not to reach absolute agreement about our ideals, but to transform *enemies* into adversaries; that is, to transform them into opponents, whose aim is *struggle*, but not mutual elimination. This may be just what the equalising, anti-idealist impulse in satire can reveal. In Smrekar's illustration of *Martin Krpan*, there is no Slovene People pitted against Imperial Authority; instead, a peasant bickers with a pretentious court. In wartime *Top Lista Nadrealista*, mythical struggles between Christianity and Islam are deflated, even if the reality of those ethnic-religious confrontations is acknowledged. Stripped of its ideological pretensions, politics in equalising satire becomes a lowly, tragicomic, unexceptional confrontation between earthly creatures.[18]

Woody De Othello, ***Warm Welcome***, 2019.

Satirical "low blows" offer no quick ideological solutions, and we would be wrong to ignore the way satire can easily flip into symbolic violence. But if we can understand satire's caustic humour as linked to a realist conception of politics, then it becomes easier to see how satire can rise above cynicism and be politically productive. Staging a confrontation between mere adversaries, satire attempts to stay a worse violence: a struggle to the death, which is predicated on the politics

17. Chantal Mouffe, *The Democratic Paradox* (London: Verso, 2005), especially pp. 101–105, 116–118.

18. We might suggest that this form of satire reveals what Emily Apter has analysed as "unexceptional" politics: behind-the-scenes wheeling and dealing, opportunistic politicking, "Machiavellianism in its modern historical mutations", which traditional political theory has tended to ignore. Emily Apter, *Unexceptional Politics* (London: Verso, 2018), p. 1.

Sacha Baron Cohen as Borat, 2006.

of ideals. The absurd realism of satire, we might say, is opposed to that divinely cruel, uncompromising, dialectical battle in which one form of Being overcomes another – be it democracy wiping out authoritarianism, world communism triumphing over capitalism, or one ethnic ideal asserting itself over all others. Yes, each real political action ultimately requires ideals, and pure *Realpolitik* is a cynical enterprise. But when a power struggle has already begun, when it has already become bloodshed, a moratorium on ideals may be the best thing that an artistic protest can offer.

And what of such satire today? The political merits of any artistic strategy must be judged from the specifics of its historical situation. A general analysis of satire cannot issue a blanket "pro" or "contra" for an entire genre. But it is hard to imagine, in 2019, a satire like *Team America* or *Borat* enjoying the kind of success that these films had in the mid-2000s. To an extent this is understandable. As hard-won ideals of tolerance become threatened by populism and xenophobia, we may rightly feel more protective of them. Simultaneously, low-attention-span media like Twitter thrive on sanctimony and outrage, and so we may feel it is safer to stay on-message. Either way, the temptation today is to draw clear battle lines and hold tightly to the views we think are right. However, what an analysis of examples like *Martin Krpan* and *Top Lista Nadrealista* offers is the thought that even satire, which attacks "our own" ideals, need not result in cynicism, but may rather keep the spirit of criticism alive. It is not the job of satire to set our moral compass, or to usher in a better world. Satire can only invite bitter laughter at the realisation that blind faith in abstract ideals exacts a price in all-too-real violence. In a world increasingly brutal and polarised, this is a reminder we would do well to heed.

BAY GANYO

Bay Ganyo is a fictional anti-hero created in the 19th-century by the writer Aleko Konstantinov (1863–1897) as a parody of an uncouth, rural Bulgarian. Ganyo serves as the simple but opportunistic protagonist in a series of satirical *feuilletons*, including *To Chicago and Back* (1894), which chronicles Konstantinov's visit to the World's Columbian Exposition in 1893, and *Bay Ganyo goes around Europe* (1895), in which Ganyo is the Other comically set against other Others throughout the Austro-Hungarian and German empires, Switzerland, and Russia, where he travels selling rose oil. Later issues depict Ganyo no longer as an entrepreneurial salesman, but a politician, satirising the political problems of post-liberation Bulgaria in the late 19th-century. Akin to Fran Levstik's Martin Krpan in Slovenia, the Czech Švejk, Tartarin of Tarascon in France, and Ostap Bender in Russia, the character has become an archetype of the lower-middle class. Konstantinov's character of Bay Ganyo was based on a real person – Ganyo Somov, a rose merchant from the village of Enina near Kazanlak; the honorific Bay is a Bulgarian term intended to signify an older or more influential person. In the ensuing century-and-a-half of nascent nationalism, Bay Ganyo has been instrumentalised by various, often opposing, parties, from right-wing extremists to progressives, modernisers to traditionalists.

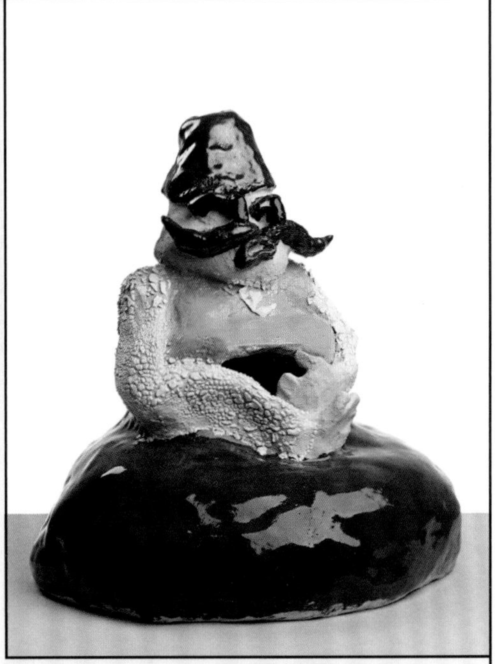

Martina Vacheva, ***Uncle Greedy***, 2018.

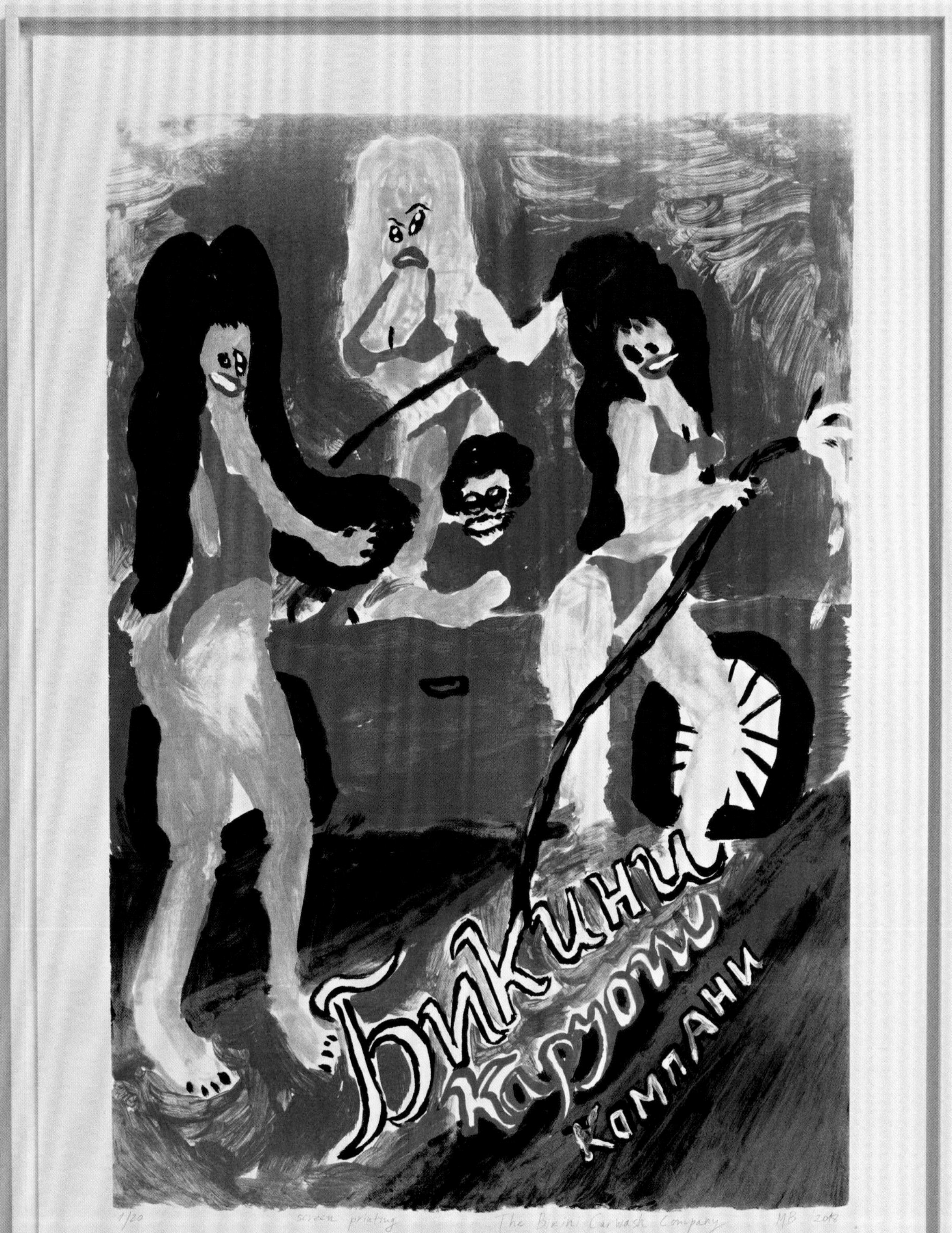

Martina Vacheva, ***The Bikini Carwash Company***, 2018. From the Print Portfolio, The 33rd Ljubljana Biennial of Graphic Arts, 2019.

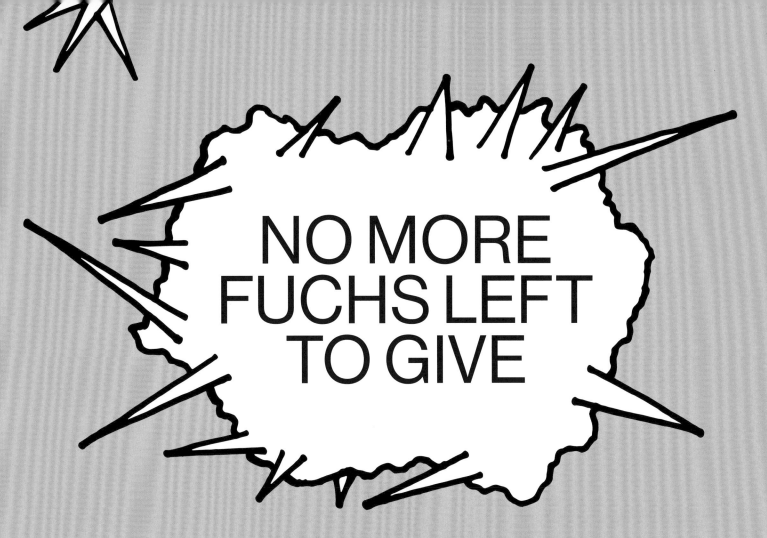

NO MORE FUCHS LEFT TO GIVE

ARTHUR FOURNIER & RAPHAEL KOENIG

Arthur Fournier & Raphael Koenig, ***No More Fuchs Left to Give***, 2019. Installation view at the 33rd Ljubljana Biennial of Graphic Arts, 2019.

Eduard Fuchs (1870–1940) was one of the most versatile and prolific figures of the German left at the turn of the century. His dual roles as a collector and critically engaged historian of lithographs helped contemporaries including Walter Benjamin (see his essay "Eduard Fuchs, Collector and Historian", 1937) grasp the role of mechanically-reproduced satirical images in the production of political discourses. Fuchs was keenly aware of the double-edged nature of such images, which can either talk back to power or reinforce existing mechanisms of oppression.

Fuchs joined the staff of the illustrated satirical fortnightly newspaper *The South German Coachman* (*Der Süddeutsche Postillon*) as editor-in-chief in 1892. This experience at the helm of a left-leaning journal piqued his interest in the popular art of lithographic caricature, which he collected voraciously.

From 1902 onwards, he published his findings in abundantly illustrated volumes featuring reproductions of prints from his private collection, accompanied by detailed socio-historical analyses that offered politically progressive takes on sensitive, hotly debated topics of the day. Such albums provided occasions for Fuchs to critically deconstruct the imagery of nationalism, militarism, gender roles, and popular representations of sexuality.

One of his most compelling works in that regard is his three-volume study *Women Domination* (*Weiberherrschaft*). For Fuchs, the pervasive iconography of female dominance – ranging from mythological depictions to dominatrix fantasies – represents a kind of symbolic compensation for the harassment and brutalities suffered by women in patriarchal societies. Such images of powerful women, Fuchs imagined, might also one day pave the way for fairer, more equal gender relations.

Fuchsen's Rückkehr.

10. August 98 — 10. Juni 99.

Zehn Monde um! Die Haft ist aus!
Froh kehrt der Redakteur nach Haus.
Es holt ihn heim mit Jubelton
Und Peitschenknall der „Postillon“.

Nichts hat die Strafe hier „genützt“ —
Schon wird die Feder neu gespitzt
Und heller nur entbrannt der Streit
Gen alle Narr,eit unsrer Zeit.

Ade! verwünschtes Mauerloch.
Ha, Kerkerwart — was willst du noch?
Der Gefängnißwärter:
„Wenn Menschen auseinander gehn,
So sagen sie: Auf Wiederseh'n!“

←
Max Engert, *Fuchs' Return* (*Fuchsen's Rückkehr*). Colour lithograph for *The South German Carriage Driver: Political-Satirical Worker's Newspaper* (*Süddeutscher Postillon: Politisch-Satirisches Arbeiterblatt*), a biweekly journal edited by Eduard Fuchs and published by M. Ernst (Munich, 1899). Engert's image shows Eduard Fuchs astride a flying beer stein, belching with zig-zag lines of anarchic energy upon his release from prison in June of 1899, revelling in the enjoyment of beer, freedom, and fresh air. Fuchs had been imprisoned for *lèse-majesté*; undeterred, he sharpens his quill to pen more anti-government materials. The prison guard below ominously waves and shouts, "We'll see each other again!" ("Es giebt ein Wiedersehen!").

S.M. Opus 731, Colour lithograph for *The South German Carriage Driver: Political-Satirical Worker's Newspaper*. The image shows a corpulent government censor in a room cluttered with seized materials. As a police officer arrives with additional journals, the censor remarks: "I've already confiscated so much, that soon, there won't be anything left to confiscate." ("Ich habe nun so viel konfisziert, das mir zu konfiszieren bald nichts mehr übrig bleibt."). The picture above the censor's desk provides the scene with a particularly grim background, showing Eduard Fuchs and another publisher executed by hanging as a symbolic, yet unambiguous reminder of the brutality of governmental repression.

Michael Myers, *Impeach Nixon*, linocut bumpersticker in black and orange on 33.6 × 13.4 cm yellow paper, i.e., second state (San Francisco: Hermes Free Press, ca. 1972). The rebus-style word puzzle spells out "IM + (peach) N + ("ick" portrait of the President gagging) + (sun)," urging members of the U.S. Senate to dipose of the disgraced leader. Under the moniker Zephyus Image, Myers and his collaborator Holbrook Teter used printmaking as a playful but potent form of political street theatre.

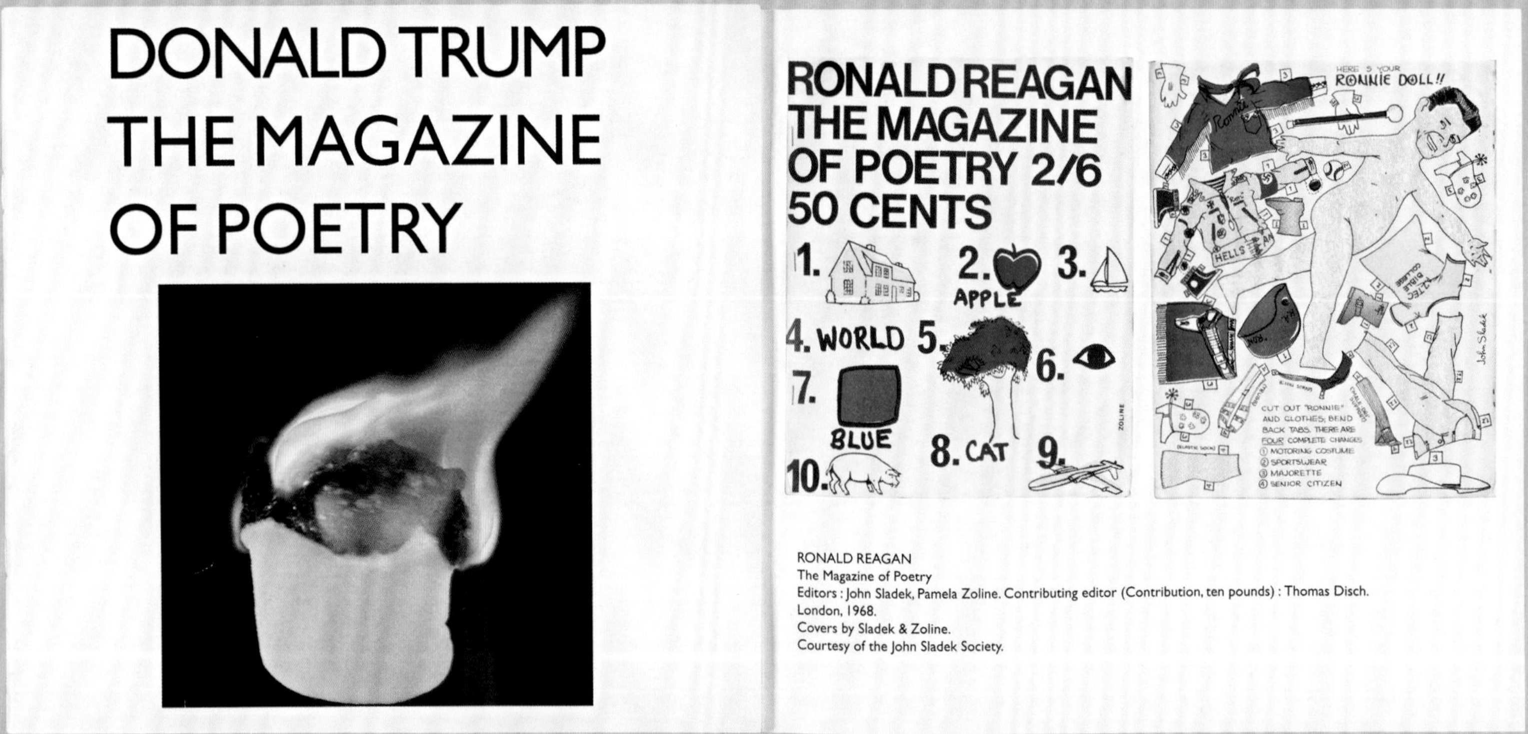

Henry Wessells, *Donald Trump The Magazine of Poetry*, offset lithographic illustrated artist's book (Upper Montclair, New Jersey: Temporary Culture, 2016.) Front cover photograph of burning marshmallow by Henry Wessells, an American poet, publisher and bookseller who responded to the election of Donald Trump with a satirical blast of words and images. Wessells acknowledged the chilling prescience of Sladek & Zoline's *Ronald Reagan The Magazine of Poetry*, No. 1 (London, 1968), by including reproductions of its covers in his own publication, thus purposefully reconnecting with the irreverent inventiveness of 1960s political graphic arts.

Albert Fiebiger, *Untitled*, colour lithograph for *The South German Carriage Driver: Political-Satirical Worker's Newspaper*. Fiebiger's image depicts the spirit of the era as a skeletal clown, coupled with the foreboding verse "Always jolly, you great Time, Jolly in your dazzling Fool's garments! Even when dancing on a Volcano – Always jolly! Because why should you care?" ("Immer Lustig, du tolle Zeit, Lustig im schillernden Narrenkleid! Tanzest du auch auf einem Vulkan – Immer lustig! Was sieht's dich an?"). The deep-seated pessimism of this allegory of the *zeitgeist* stands in sharp contrast with the usual iconography of the *Postillon*, which often expressed more confidence in the journal's socially progressive agenda.

Joseph Kuhn-Régnier, *Aristotle and Phyllis*, lithograph (Paris, 1910). Reproduced in E. Fuchs, *Weiberherrschaft*, Vol. 1, No. 35. The apocryphal story of Aristotle and Phyllis is a cautionary tale of the limits of rationalism: as Aristotle was advising Alexander the Great to leave his lover Phyllis, the latter took revenge on Aristotle by seducing him and convincing him to engage in a BDSM encounter *avant la lettre*. She then proceeded to ride him like a horse, arranging for Alexander to witness the scene, thus putting his teacher and one of the founding fathers of Western philosophy in an incongruous and rather undignified position. As an illustrator of pedagogical works on Greek and Roman antiquity and a successful caricaturist, Joseph Kuhn-Régnier (1873–1940) was uniquely qualified to offer this lively, Belle Époque take on an ancient iconographic trope.

→
Auguste Roedel (1859–1900), *The Mad Cow*, colour lithograph (Paris, 1897). Reproduced in E. Fuchs, *Weiberherrschaft*, Vol. 2, No. 424, under the title "The Satisfied Torera". Originally published as a cover of the French satirical illustrated magazine *The Mad Cow* (*La Vache enragée*) as an advertisement for the *Vachalcade* or "Promenade of the Mad Cow", a carnival procession of the Montmartre district that functioned as a rallying point for artists and writers of the Paris "bohème" in the 1880s and 1890s. In the *Weiberherrschaft*, Fuchs puts the motive in parallel with the biblical episode of Judith beheading Holofernes.

←
Master B.R., *Aristotle and Campaspe*, etching (Netherlands, late 15th-century). Reproduced in E. Fuchs, *Weiberherrschaft*, Vol. 2, No. 595. "Campaspe" is sometimes used as an alternative name for Phyllis. In the *Weiberherrschaft*, Fuchs offers a large selection of graphic interpretations of the story of Aristotle and Phyllis, ranging from 12th-century Romanesque stone carvings to modern times. He also dwells on the impressive international extension of its mechanisms of diffusion, from a 2nd-century Sanskrit original to medieval French and German ballads through Persian, Arabic, Hebrew, and Latin translations. Master B.R.'s version is particularly remarkable for Aristotle's ambiguous gaze, directed straight at the viewer, either emphasising the philosopher's confusion of being caught in the act or attempting to make the viewer into a complicit voyeur.

Jean-Adolphe Lafosse, *Truncated Claws*, lithograph (Paris, 1850). Reproduced in E. Fuchs, *Weiberherrschaft*, Vol. 2, No. 361. Partly derived from an 1836 painting by Camille Roqueplan, this motif is based on Aesop's cautionary tale "The Lion in Love" (Fable 140), later adapted by Jean de La Fontaine. Lafosse innovates by emphasising the underlying erotic and psychological tensions of the scene: the lion's fiancée's bare breasts seem to invite a predatory male gaze, which is simultaneously repelled and symbolically castrated by a large pair of scissors at the centre of the composition. It is fair to assume that, when publishing the second volume of the *Weiberherrschaft* in 1913, Fuchs' choice of displaying Lafosse's lithograph in a prominent position was informed by Freud's early writings on the castration complex (1908) and on scopophilia or *Schautrieb* (1905).

MONTMARTRE
Nlle ATHÈNES
ROEDEL

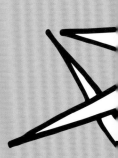

Jean Veber, *Marianne's Footstep*, colour lithograph, ed. Edmond Sagot (Paris, 1905). Reproduced in E. Fuchs, *Weiberherrschaft*, Vol. 1, No. 175. Jean Veber (1864–1928) was a leading caricaturist of the late 19th-century, and a regular contributor to the illustrated newspaper *Le Rire* (*Laughter*). Fuchs included his vivid depiction of Marianne (the allegorical impersonation of the French Republic) on the basis of its artistic merits and thematic relevance, linking state power with a strong, even violent female body, but was far from endorsing its political message. Fuchs and Veber stood at opposite ends of the political spectrum, as Veber's arch-conservative portrayal of an unhinged, red-faced Marianne was meant to constitute a vitriolic critique of the "plebeian" Republic's perceived assault on Catholic values in the context of the hotly debated 1905 law that abolished all ties between the French state and religious institutions.

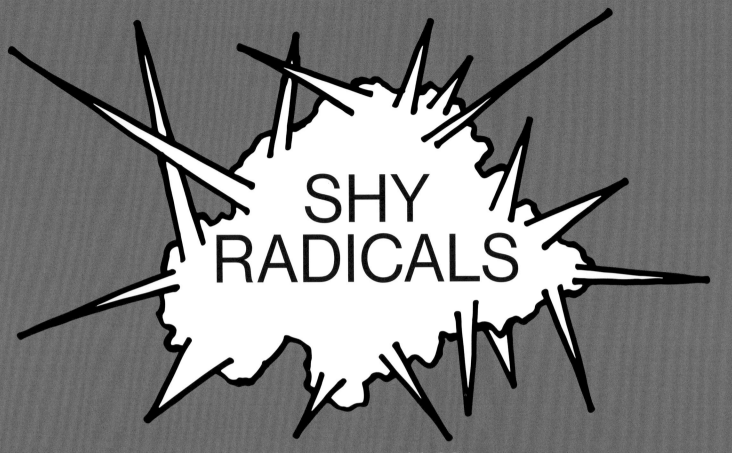

SHY RADICALS

THE ANTISYSTEMIC POLITICS OF THE MILITANT INTROVERT

HAMJA AHSAN

The quieter you become,
the more you are able to hear.
—Lao Tzu

Drawing together communiqués, covert interviews, and the oral and underground histories of introvert struggles, Hamja Ahsan's *Shy Radicals* provides a detailed documentation of the political demands of shy people.

Radicalised against the imperial domination of globalised PR projectionism, extrovert poise, and loudness, the Shy Radicals and their guerrilla wing – the Shy Underground – are a vanguard movement intent on trans-rupting the consensus extrovert-supremacist politics and assertiveness culture of the 21st-century. The movement aims to establish an independent homeland – Aspergistan, a utopian state for introverted people, run according to Shyria Law and underpinned by Pan-Shyist ideology, protecting the rights of the oppressed, quiet, and shy people.

Shy Radicals are the Black Panther Party of the introvert class, and their anti-systemic manifesto is a quiet and thoughtful polemic, a satire that uses anti-colonial theory to build a critique of dominant culture and the rising tide of Islamophobia.

Seashell, the national anthem of the Shy People's Republic of Aspergistan.

THE ASPERGISTAN REFERENDUM, 2019

On the occasion of the 33rd Biennial of Graphic Arts, a referendum on secession asks the exhibition venues in Ljubljana to join the breakaway Aspergistan Federation: the national homeland of Shy, Introvert, and Autistic spectrum peoples as constituted in the book *Shy Radicals*. From ballot boxes to a national anthem and social media hashtags, the Aspergistan Referendum continues Ahsan's interest in what he calls a "global Introfada struggle against Extrovert-supremacy." The vibrant civil society of post-socialist, post-Yugoslav Slovenia offers a particularly apt context for an investigation of how introspection, identity, and affect collide.

Join the conversation and follow the hashtags #VoteAspergistan.

Join the struggle and post the #ShyPower salute in various locations.

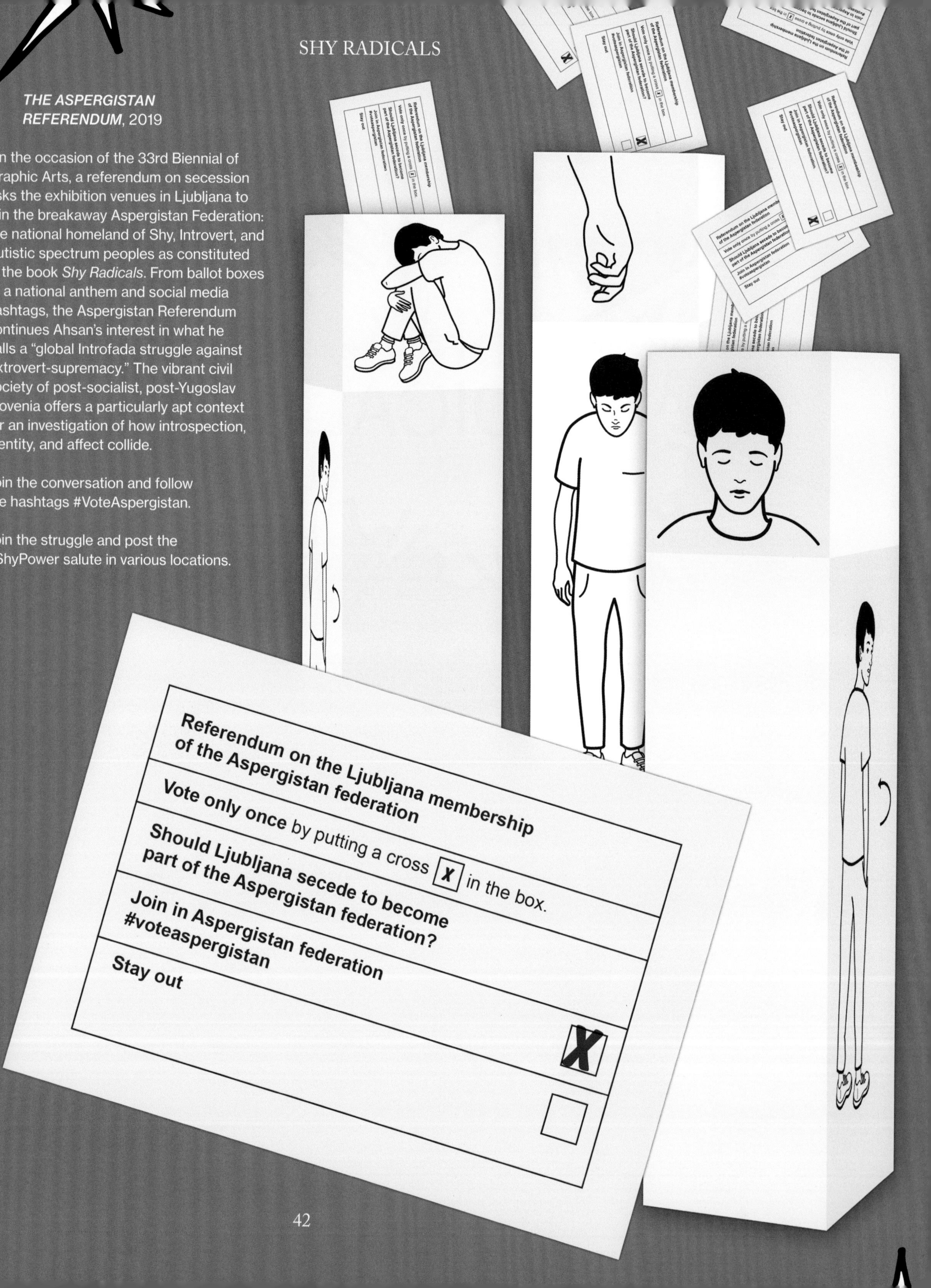

Referendum on the Ljubljana membership of the Aspergistan federation
Vote only once by putting a cross X in the box.
Should Ljubljana secede to become part of the Aspergistan federation?
Join in Aspergistan federation #voteaspergistan
Stay out
X

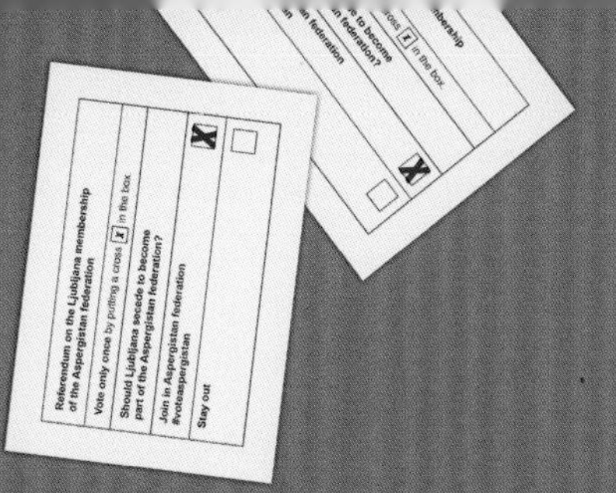

→
Hamja Ahsan, ***Shy Radicals: The Antisystemic Politics of the Militant Introvert***, 2017. Design and illustrations by Rose Nordin.

SHY PEOPLE'S REPUBLIC OF ASPERGISTAN

WE, THE PEOPLES OF ASPERGISTAN,

EMBODY THE SHY PEOPLES REPUBLIC OF ASPERGISTAN– the sanctuary, beacon and homeland of oppressed Shy, Introvert and Autistic Spectrum peoples – and understand that our nation's crowning principles will serve as a bulwark against the hegemony of the Extrovert World Order, marking a decisive step toward the fraternal and sororal collaboration and co-existence of all Shy Peoples in an autonomous worldwide union.

ACKNOWLEDGE that successive generations of our people have suffered rejection, bullying, humiliation, belittlement, pathologisation, persecution, subjugation, exploitation, erasure, exclusion, alienation, discrimination and disadvantage at the hands of the global system of Extrovert-Supremacism, which has dispossessed and deprived us of our right to introspective life, self-esteem, equality and peace.

DEMAND the reversal of the operations of Extrovert-exclusive representation in congress and debate-chamber parliaments, acknowledging the system's failure to listen to and represent its subjects and citizens. We take Lao Tzu's dictum 'the quieter you become, the more you are able to hear' as the foundational principle of our democratic institutions.

CHERISH the richness of inner life – silence, contemplation, reflective solitude, intimate company, investigative depths, peer-reviewed truth – which forms the basis and legitimacy of the state and government to determine our destiny.

On behalf of the Governing Authority of the Aspergistan Federation, it's a pleasure to announce the results of the 2019 Aspergistan Referendum, Ljubljana. Thanks to all those who voted. There was an excellent turnout of 575 active voters.

The Aspergistan Referendum results were announced on 27 September 2019 at 3:00 PM. The Amendment was passed by a majority of votes.

Join in Aspergistan Federation: 414 votes
72%
Stay out: 144 votes
25.04%
Invalid: 17 votes
2.96%

Hamja Ahsan, ***The Aspergistan Referendum***, 2019. Installation view at the 33rd Ljubljana Biennial of Graphic Arts, 2019.

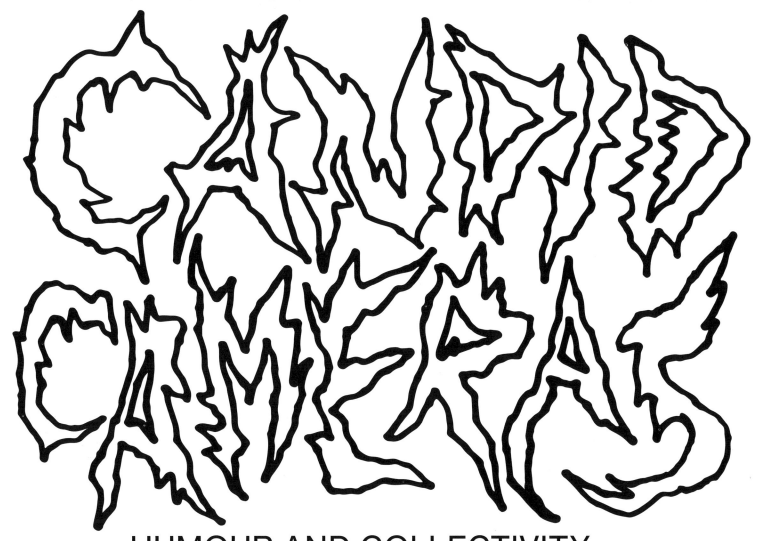

CANDID CAMERAS

HUMOUR AND COLLECTIVITY IN DARK TIMES

M. CONSTANTINE

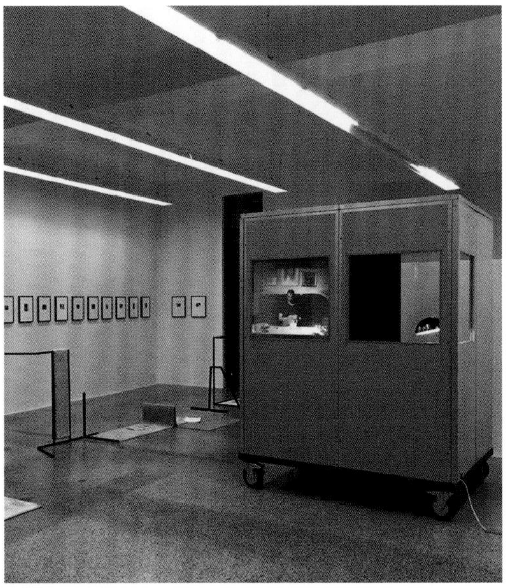

Clarissa Thieme, ***VREMEPLOV / TIME MACHINE***, 2018.

I'm standing near a small pavilion at the end of an otherwise empty parking lot in (former East) Berlin. Once a gatehouse for the old Ostbahnhof train station, the pavilion has recently begun its new life as the site of various art interventions, a common enough fate. Today it's being used as a translator's booth in a performative artwork called *VREMEPLOV / TIME MACHINE* by the artist Clarissa Thieme. In it, nearly a dozen translators are sounding live translations of dialogue from a home video created during the siege of Sarajevo. A breeze is blowing the screen on which an image is projected: it's a shitty VHS recording, full of lovely technical glitches, scrolling bands of fuzz, early graphic effects, articulated pixels, washed-out faces, and in-camera edits. Some boys in Sarajevo are joking around, but seriously looking for a way out of the war. *Today is 11th June, 1993. The war has been going on for very long. I've tried everything to get out, to save myself, nothing worked. The only thing left is to make this videotape that I will give to my son, and he to his, and so on, until a time machine is invented and someone watching it will come and get me out of this situation.* They play it straight until they break, lapsing into a tender, fraternalistic horseplay; their laughter

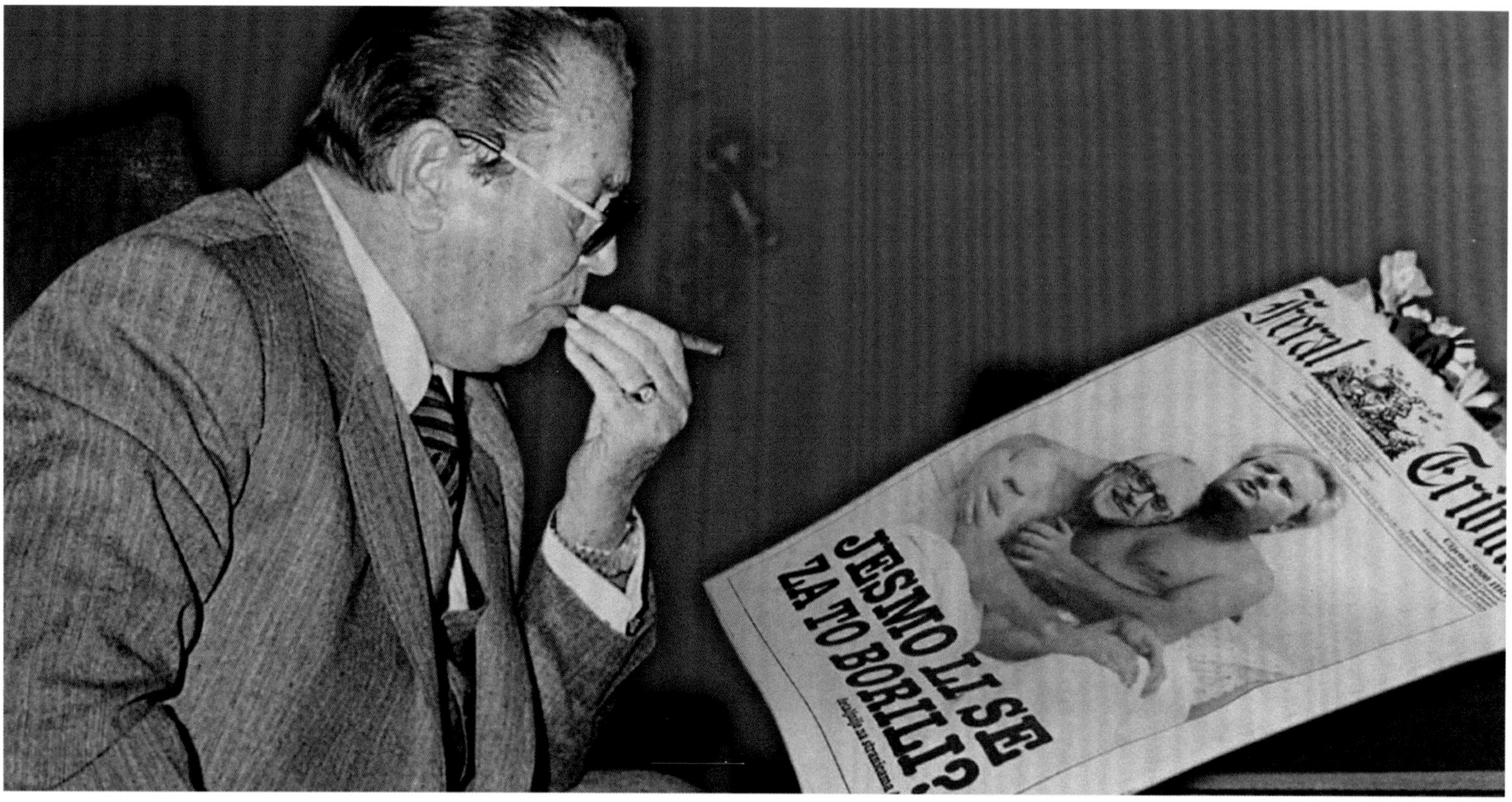

Josip Broz Tito reading the Croatian satirical journal ***Feral Tribune***, featuring an intimate look at Croatian and Serbian Presidents Franjo Tuđman and Slobodan Milošević.

is contagious. In the video, they are speaking Bosnian.[1] And in this parking lot, in the night heat, a crowd of people is standing around buying beers out of the trunk of a car, listening to live translations of the video as it plays over and over. It is translated with the kind of deadpan, affect-less delivery common to voiceover translation practices throughout Eastern Europe,[2] into a dozen or so prominent languages spoken in Berlin. In spite of all the translation work, it's funny to think that most people here, most of the time, are listening to words they don't understand. Even when they do, translations always want for a better fidelity. But we're here, laughing along with these guys, amidst the languages we don't understand, through a document of a situation we can't possibly imagine. And yet, on *some* visceral level, we get it. In this parking lot, on this night, we're receiving a broadcast to the future-present.

The video is a weird genre-bend that arcs through sci-fi, satire, and wartime docu-drama. It is both a fantasy and a means of survival, a rescue narrative by way of patriarchal futurism and technological retrogression. And it is a document of play, friendship, and the necessary work of humour, used to break the tension of imposed captivity and the threat of sniper warfare that became the new quotidian normal during the siege. The video opens with a single shot of a boy in his early 20s, sitting on a sofa, looking into the camera and giving a sincere and humourless plea to an unknown addressee in a distant future: *Today is 11th June, 1993. The war has been going on for very long …* As he ends his entreaty, a seamless in-camera cut suddenly materialises another young man beside him: *Hey, who are you?* The rescuer says, *I saw the tape and*

1. Formerly known as Serbo-Croatian and predominantly similar in its spoken and written forms but with the marked inclusion of Turkish, Arabic, and Persian words, Bosnian was recognised in its modern form during the 1990s.

2. See David Crowley's article, "Echo Translation", in Slavs and Tatars, *Mirrors for Princes* (New York: NYU Abu Dhabi Art Gallery and Zürich: JRP|Ringier, 2015).

The DeLorean time machine.

I've arrived from the year 2037, to which our central character replies, *How did you get here so fast?* (Classic time-travel humour.) The rescuer starts pressing buttons on a small prop (a spare mini VHS cassette) and says, *Here, I brought this device, to bring you back to the year 2037.* But alas: in an instant their elation turns to despair when the device fails. The camera cuts to black and opens on the same couch with a different actor: *Today is 11th June, 1993. The war has been going on for very long …* This time, a traveller from the year 2320 shows up, with more advanced technology – but suffers the same failure. The video cycles through several takes, and finally, in the last scene, a traveller from the year 2572 joins our main character, along with the two previous failed time-travellers. He admonishes them for failing their missions – *You are a disgrace to the technology of your generations* – and banishes them from the couch. He assures our main character that they will escape in the superior time machine he has just arrived in, which features an improved status field and battery pack. He asks first, *Do you really want to come to my year?* And our friend replies, *Any year will do. Does it hurt?* The hero from the future gets to work on his device and suddenly – our wartime friend disappears (using the in-camera cut) – but he remains. *What happened? … I'm all alone.* He turns the camera off.

TRIO Sarajevo, ***Wake Up, Europe!***, 1993.

U.S. President Bill Clinton speaking with Bosnian President Alija Izetbegović through an interpreter, Tuzla, Bosnia, 1997.

With its particular ways of condensing and distributing tension, sharpness, and dissonance, satire often serves as a more effective conduit for tragedy than drama. The refrain *Today is 11th June …* signals the temporality and repetition of waiting through the seemingly interminable nightmare of the siege, just as it mimes comedic call-back structure. The rearticulated plea for rescue suggests the actual repeated requests for UN and intervention, arms, and humanitarian aid

Dušan Petričič, ***Bosnian Childhood***, 1994.

during the four years of embattlement and embargo imposed on the city.[3] And the recursion of technical failure in spite of hopeful visitors from increasingly distant futures reinforces the very intractability of their situation; in the end, our friend escapes, but not without the sacrifice of three others. In its tone and style, the video seems to riff on the popular Sarajevan sketch comedy show *Top Lista Nadrealista*, but equally recalls *Waiting for Godot* – a production of which, only months later, Susan Sontag was to direct (contentiously) at the MESS International Theatre Festival.[4] Throughout the video there are outtakes where the actors break into laughter, out of character, and through the fourth wall. The sci-fi tropes of time-travel and technical glitch drive the recursive narrative, always wavering between Beckettian absurdity and a genuine desire for rescue and reparation.[5]

* * *

Satisfaction video meme by Russian builder cadets, 2018.

"At some crisis times", writes Lauren Berlant, "politics is defined by a collectively held sense that a glitch has appeared in the reproduction of life." During such times, she suggests, infrastructures of relation emerge – provisional yet intimate social bonds, technologies, forms of representation, and distinct shared imaginaries – that "let a collectivity stay bound to the ordinary even as some of its forms of life are fraying, wasting …"[6] Berlant is thinking here about long-term, corrosive forms of "glitch" such as contemporary austerity politics, and the violences of immigration policy and occupation. And though the word is hardly commensurate with the war crimes perpetrated in Sarajevo (the magnitude and speed of unfolding crisis matters for what percentage of the ordinary remains to hold fast to and how), it is a useful concept that works metonymically in the narrative of the wartime sci-fi video to grow the "infrastructural" – that is, to cohere provisional forms of collectivity that

3. As reported by Nihad Kreševljaković, "U.S. President Bill Clinton was called 'Bil-ne bil' by Sarajevans because of his constant demur regarding a military intervention. [Bil in Bosnian can be translated as 'should I.' 'Bil-ne bil' roughly translates to 'should I or should I not']." *Al Jazeera Balkans*, 22 November 2015.

4. *Waiting for Godot* has been produced numerous times in dire contexts that refract its content, including multiple performances throughout apartheid South Africa, and by the artist Paul Chan in post-Katrina New Orleans, 2007.

5. Robert Zemeckis' 1998 film *Back to the Future* is a lighter example; Octavia Butler's 1979 novel *Kindred* innovates across genres of sci-fi, historical novel, grim fantasy, and slave narrative to explore the effects of race, gender, and power in intimate relations, as the main character is shuttled in time between the antebellum South and 1970s California.

6. We can spot the relationship between affect, technology, and collectivity in many times and places. Masha Gessen recently reported on the life of a video meme in Russia, in which a group of cadets filmed and inadvertently published a homoerotic parody of a satirical music video, "Satisfaction", by musician Benny Benassi. The video went viral, and as the cadets faced the threat of persecution, dozens of anonymous and allied groups began creating and posting their own "Satisfaction" video parodies. By deploying the signifiers of homoeroticism, the solidarity created among the videos helped to distribute risk differently across social strata, deferring and diluting the initial threat from the cadets to sauna-goers, retirees, nurses, EMTs, athletes, and agricultural workers. "How Russia's Hilarious, Homoerotic 'Satisfaction' Became a Meme of Solidarity", in *New Yorker*, 22 January 2018.

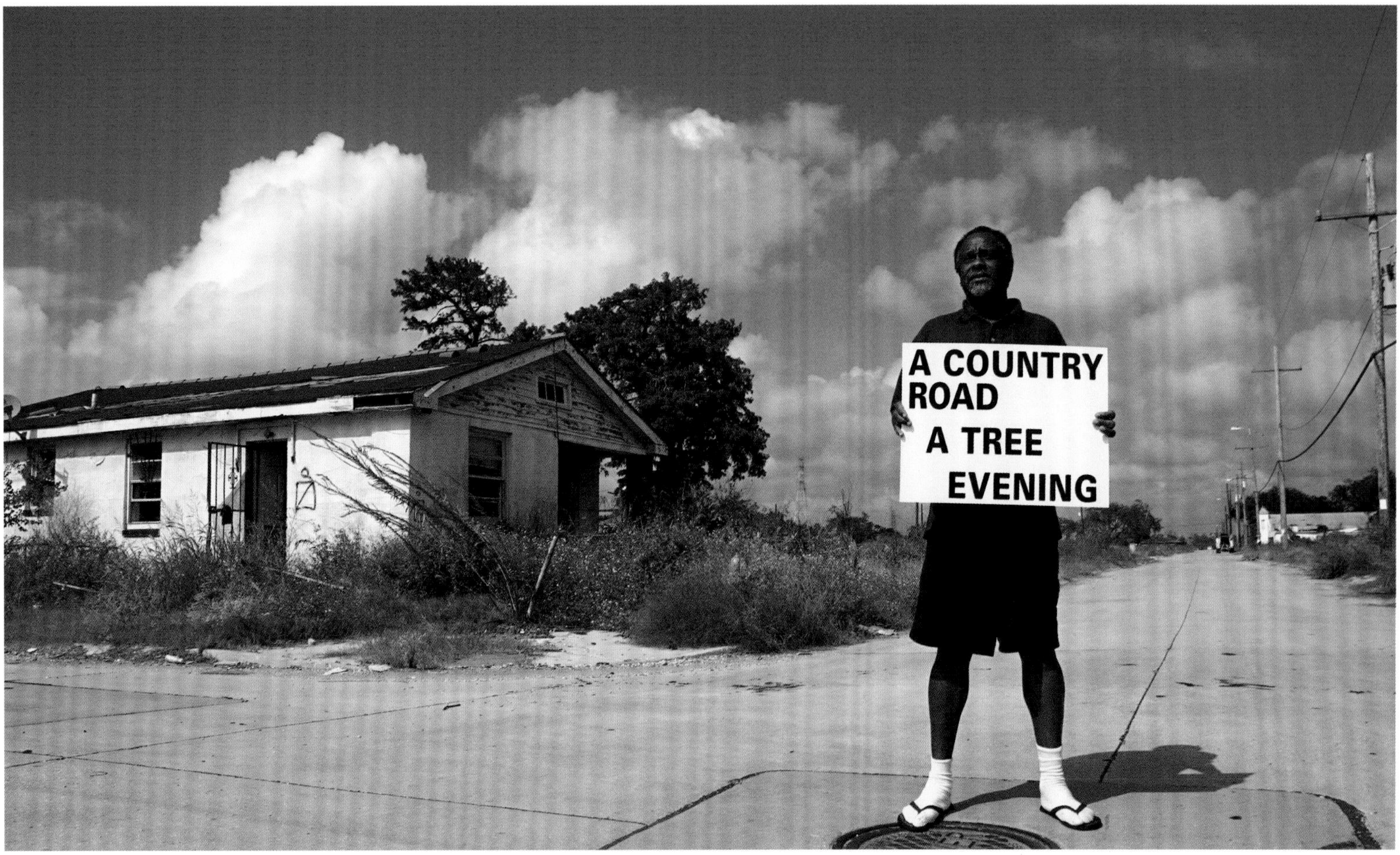

Paul Chan, ***Untitled (After Robert Lynn Green Sr.)***, 2006. Photograph accompanying Chan's production of *Waiting for Godot* in New Orleans.

> *... forge an imaginary for managing the meanwhile within damaged life's perdurance, a meanwhile that is less an end or an ethical scene than a technical political heuristic that allows for ambivalence, distraction, antagonism and inattention not to destroy collective existence. ... The question of politics becomes identical with the reinvention of infrastructures for managing the unevenness, ambivalence, violence, and ordinary contingency of contemporary existence.*[7]

Even as the ordinary was assaulted on all fronts, the sci-fi video shows a politics of survival and perdurance in its ever-provisional making. Its technology – the video camera itself (more reliable than the time machine; or is it the time machine?) – becomes part of the political infrastructure, revealing the irruption and incongruities of everyday life, and at the same time trying to preserve *some* sense of normalcy. Its affects, not least the comedic, create the galvanising mood we feel across social bonds, through the tempo and editing style, in the shaky frame destabilised by the cameraman's laughter.

The camcorder initially entered the US market in 1985, and by its second year in production doubled its unit sales to one million.[8] As free markets gradually opened across Eastern Europe in the early 1990s, sales of consumer electronics (camcorders, colour televisions, CD players) helped drive economic growth in spite of currency volatility.[9] The camcorder became an important

7. Lauren Berlant, "The commons: Infrastructures for troubling times" in *Environment and Planning D: Society and Space*, Vol. 34 (3), p. 394.

8. "Camcorder, CD Sales May Double in 1986" in *New York Times*, 2 June 1986.

9. See Andrew E. Fletcher, *The European Electronics Industry Towards 1992: A Profile of Market Leaders* (Elsevier Science Publishers Ltd., 1991).

Pablo Bronstein, ***Plečnik decorative scheme confusing some interior and exterior architectural features***, 2019. Installation view at the 33rd Ljubljana Biennial of Graphic Arts, 2019.

I CLEARLY REMEMBER THE FIRST JOKE I HEARD, A FEW MONTHS AFTER THE ATTACKS ON THE CITY HAD STARTED. THIS WAS A PERIOD OF INTENSE SNIPER SHOOTING AND THE BEGINNING OF CIGARETTE SHORTAGES.

MUJO AND SULJO (RECURRING CHARACTERS IN BOSNIAN JOKES) ARE RUNNING ACROSS A ROAD. SUDDENLY, A SNIPER BULLET SEVERS MUJO'S EAR!

MUJO RETURNS TO THE MIDDLE OF THE ROAD AND STARTS LOOKING FOR SOMETHING WHILE BULLETS FLY ALL AROUND HIM.

REALISING THAT HE IS LOOKING FOR HIS EAR, SULJO SHOUTS: *FORGET THE EAR, THE SNIPER WILL KILL YOU.*

MUJO REPLIES: *I DON'T CARE ABOUT THE EAR, BUT I HAD A CIGARETTE STUCK BEHIND IT.*

device to forge new markets, and gave citizens a way of making and entering history through documentation of political changes and social transformation. Results of product R&D and consumer testing led manufacturers to privilege a reduction in camera size, ease of use, and increased portability over image quality; Sony's lightweight, revolutionary Handycam was touted as "perfect for people on the go."[10] Thus the 'shitty' aesthetic and visual noise that provokes nostalgia today (especially amidst ever more smooth virtual realities) was a result of deliberately under-engineered light capture technologies. Yet improvements in VHS and integrated microphones from earlier generations of 8mm and 16mm home film cameras allowed audio data to be captured, rendering more sensorially rich environments. In a pocket of history after the Cold War and before the internet, the early 1990s was a seminal time in media; widespread use of portable recording devices presaged the social transformations and political power that smartphones would bring a decade later. But then, as now, broader corporate flows, market diagnostics, and technical proficiencies in certain corners of the globe set conditions of possibility for the aesthetics and pragmatics of mediated social formations elsewhere.

VREMEPLOV was in fact one among many home videos created during the siege. Encouraged in part by the televised request of municipal police chief Dragan Vikić in the early months of warfare, residents of Sarajevo took up their home video cameras as weapons. As one of the tactical measures he suggested alongside organising citizen militia defence groups, Vikić implored, "I would really like to ask you to appeal, if you can, to all citizens who own video cameras to start filming, as their material will definitely have an effect."[11] The need to record derived as much from an understanding of how the siege was being perceived – or rather misrepresented – in the international media, as from an impulse to document the incomprehensible destruction of their

The 1985 Sony Video 8 AF Handycam is the first of its kind to have an 8mm cassette recording feature.

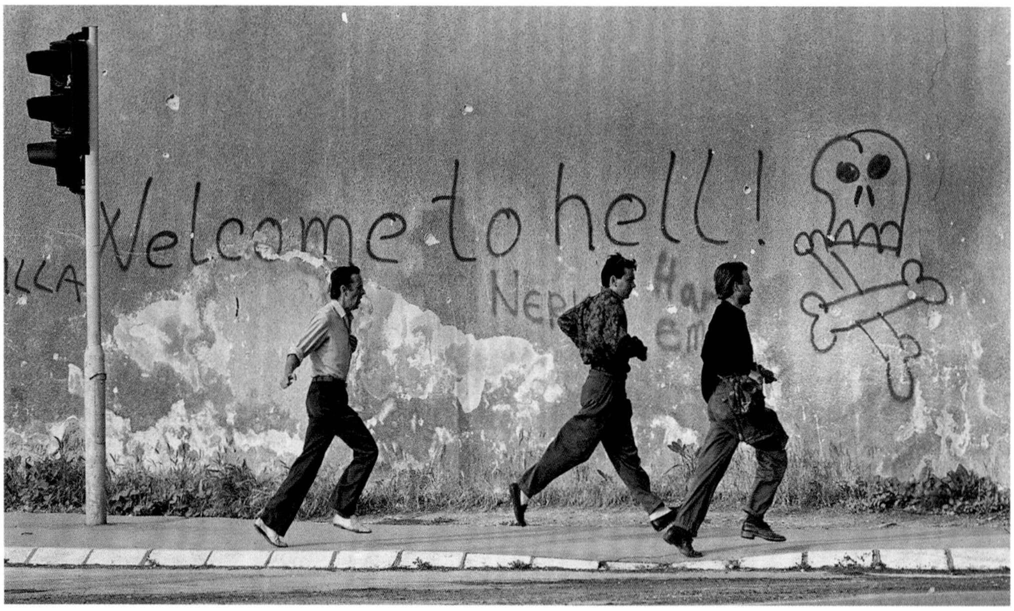

Three men run for cover as sniper fire rings out along Sarajevo's notorious "sniper alley", Wednesday, 9 June 1993.

10. Sony Annual Report 1990, p. 6. https://www.sony.net/SonyInfo/IR/library/ar/1990-E.pdf. Accessed 17 May 2019.

11. Nihad Kreševljaković and Sead Kreševljaković, *Do you remember Sarajevo?* film, 2003.

Street sign for Susan Sontag Square, Sarajevo, Bosnia and Herzegovina.

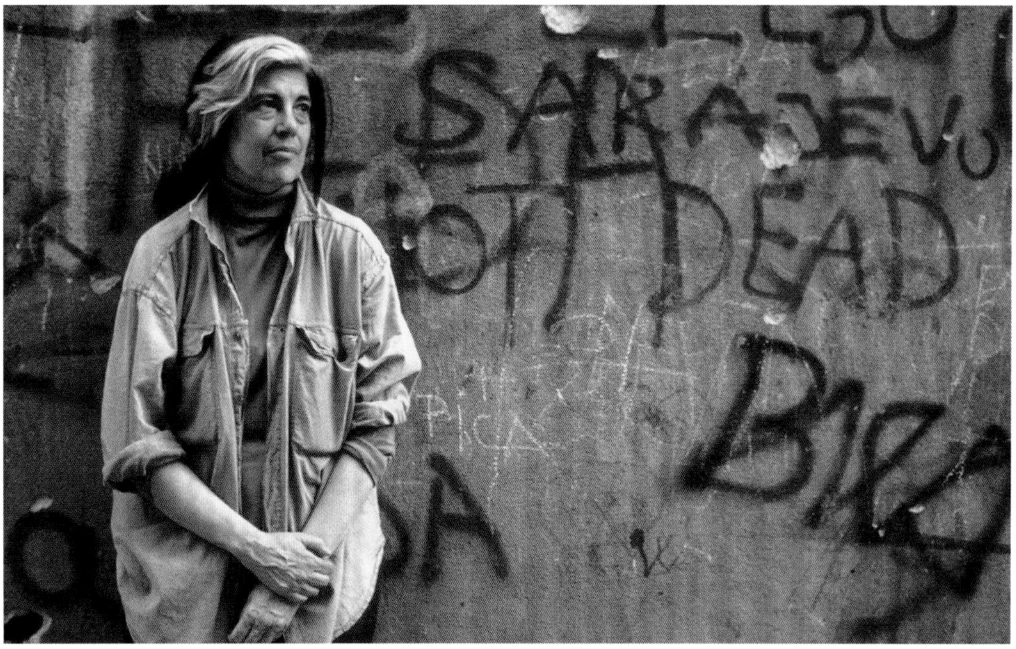

Susan Sontag in Sarajevo, Bosnia and Herzegovina, 1993.

lives and realities.[12] Sounds of air sirens, shellings, laughter, breath, gunfire, broken glass and rubble underfoot, shouts, shock, music, and calls to prayer were among some of the more salient sonic details recorded by residents of Sarajevo during the siege. These populate and punctuate documentation of attacks, television news broadcasts, domestic scenes of boredom, hunger, and cold, children playing, funerals, weddings, sniper brigades, comical skits, makeshift medical care, mosques, and vulnerable food lines that comprised residents' everyday lives. Flipping the script of journalistic media through which the conflict was otherwise portrayed, the footage is largely narrated by the exclamations of citizens: *They've burned Mojmilo Hall?!* [the cinema]; *Feels the same as '41 …*; and – not without a little dark humour – *Don't be afraid! There are no snipers here … only mortars … hahaha.* Minor but poignant roles are played by politicians and diplomats; British Foreign Secretary and peace negotiator David Owen makes a brief appearance with his famously patronising address to Bosnians, "Don't dream dreams".[13] The double-layer of representation – a video recording of a TV broadcast – stresses the sense of remove and alienation at being the third party non-addressee in public performances of British tough-love diplomacy.

Indeed, as Sontag later recalled, French philosopher Andre Glucksmann had argued that "the war would be won or lost not by anything that happened in Sarajevo, or indeed in Bosnia, but by what happened in the media."[14] Sontag characterised the dissolution of Yugoslavia and conflict in Bosnia as "the Spanish Civil War of our time", and admonished America's intellectual elite for their conspicuous absence too, suggesting that it was not fear of danger that kept them away,[15] but something more ominous, a "failure of conscience".[16] Pervasive "Balkanism" and Islamophobia – on behalf of politicians, journalists, and intellectuals – also didn't go unnoticed.[17] Though her production of *Godot* was widely and vituperatively panned in Western media,[18] Sontag's presence in

12. Contemporary, post-internet media collectives such as Abounaddara (Syria), Active Stills (Israel / Palestine), and the Karrabing Film Collective (Australia) work in analogous ways, intervening in representations of war, political conflict, and extractive capital, and creating critical concepts and practices.

13. Clarissa Thieme reflects on the significance of this statement and the effect it had on Sarajevans' sense of temporality and waiting in an interview with Jana Seehusen, "About the 'Feeling of Being in Transition'" in *Temporary Art Review*, 25 September 2018.

14. Susan Sontag, *Regarding the Pain of Others* (New York: Picador, 2003), p. 84. See also "Waiting for Godot in Sarajevo", in *Performing Arts Journal* 16:2 (1994). Sontag contrasts her own involvement to that of Glucksmann and other French intellectuals, referring to them as "day-trippers" to Sarajevo during the war years.

15. Sontag would die in 2004, after living with disease for the better part of three decades. One can speculate whether her experience of prolonged illness changed her sensitivity to risk.

16. John F. Burns, "To Sarajevo, Writer Brings Good Will and 'Godot'" in *New York Times*, 19 August 1993.

17. See the critical texts of Milica Bakić-Hayden, "Nesting Orientalisms: The Case of Former Yugoslavia" in *Slavic Review* 54:4 (1995); and Maria Todarova, *Imagining the Balkans* (Oxford: Oxford University Press, 1997).

18. These reviews were from the same journalists who were on assignment covering the war. Sontag would encounter them during her stay at the Holiday Inn, the only functioning hotel in Sarajevo at the time.

Sarajevo was warmly received – she was even awarded honorary citizenship by the mayor. Haris Pašović, a collaborator and producer of the play, evaded Serbian gunfire in order to return to the city. "We want to make our lives as normal as possible", he said, "We want our work to be impeccable."[19] Actress Ines Fančović, who played the role of Pozo, stated, "Acting is a kind of therapy for me. If I didn't work almost every day I would find it very difficult to live through this war. The shelling and the death of many friends so far has shaken me, but acting helps me forget."[20] As schools, cinemas, and other cultural institutions were subject to targeted attacks, music, movies, and theatre continued in makeshift, bombed-out spaces. Though the intent of the home videos was to intervene in representations of the war, to solicit humanitarian and military aid, they became artefacts of a broader effort to preserve culture and its making through dark times.

Sachiko Kazama, ***War-Pup***, 2005.

Stane Jagodič, ***Memorial of Sarajevo Martyrs***, 1992.

* * *

Several characters from the *VREMEPLOV* video played key roles in this cultural preservation, and were instrumental in holding a tenuous continuity over a longer historical arc. As residents of Sarajevo amassed thousands of hours of documentary footage throughout the siege, twin brothers Nihad and Sead Kreševljaković gave up the basement of their family home as a holding space for this material. After the siege ended in 1995, they continued to be the unofficial archivists of the city's witness to itself. In the decade that followed, the brothers began poring through the videos, and eventually started compiling and editing the footage into what would become their documentary *Do You Remember Sarajevo?*. Friend and writer Chris Keulemans describes their process:

19. Burns, "To Sarajevo".

20. As told to Kevin Weaver, "Culture under siege", *The Stage*, 25 August 1993.

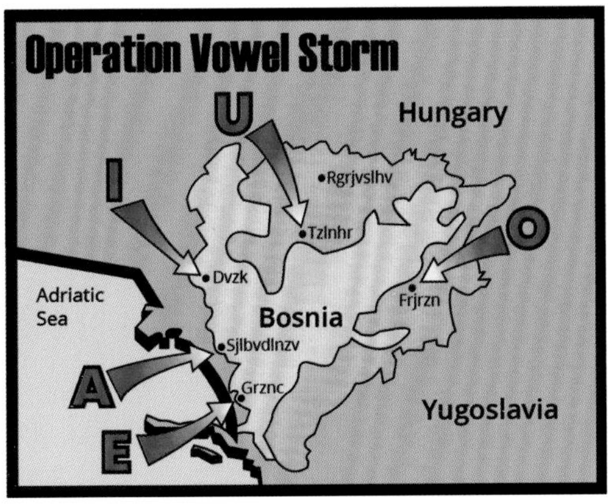

Before an emergency joint session of Congress yesterday, President Clinton announced U.S. plans to deploy over 75,000 vowels to the war-torn region of Bosnia. The deployment, the largest of its kind in American history, will provide the region with the critically needed letters A, E, I, O and U, and is hoped to render countless Bosnian names more pronounceable.

The deployment, dubbed Operation Vowel Storm by the State Department, is set for early next week, with the Adriatic port cities of Sjlbvdnzv and Grzny slated to be the first recipients. Two C-130 transport planes, each carrying over 500 24-count boxes of "E's," will fly from Andrews Air Force Base across the Atlantic and airdrop the letters over the cities.

The airdrop represents the largest deployment of any letter to a foreign country since 1984. During the summer of that year, the U.S. shipped 92,000 consonants to Ethiopia, providing cities like Ouaouoaua, Eaoiiuae, and Aao with vital, life-giving supplies of L's, S's and T's.
–*The Onion*, December 1995

Every evening around midnight, they would descend into the basement to view material, select fragments and do rough edits. The only problem was: they never systematically ordered all those tapes, and dreamers as they were, they didn't care. Which meant that they would more or less start all over again every night. At first, I thought this was traumatized madness, even though they approached their work with cheerful, boundless energy. Every time I visited, they would proudly take me down to the basement, tell me that they had – again – barely made any progress – and laugh their irresistible laughs as if this was the best joke in the world.[21]

Time and repeated overdubbing would create generational loss through the deterioration of the magnetic film in which video and audio data had been encoded. But in important ways, the Kreševljaković brothers created opportunities for memory – however unstable – to be preserved and shared. As the years passed and Sarajevans who fled the city during the siege began to return, the brothers organised screenings of the home videos. These doubled as a way of retelling histories. They offered a place to express guilt for those who left, and to work trauma and anger for those who stayed. They underscored new social rifts and unlikely solidarities borne of the conflict.

Do You Remember Sarajevo? was completed ten years after *VREMEPLOV*, in 2003. It stands as a singular document of a city under siege and an indictment of regional perpetrators and their international conspirators. The editing plays with poetic visual riffs and rhyme schemes across the fragmented footage; sound is often deliberately mis-synchronised. There are repeated scenes of someone filming from the windows while a friend or family member behind them tells them to get away from the windows because … *it's a sniper*, or … *they're shelling.* In an instant, the orthography of the frame drops, shakes, succumbs to the need to navigate a dangerous environment. This makes the risk of seeing and shooting (footage) palpable. Betraying the comedic sensibilities of the editors, short skits feature amongst scenes of everyday violence. After a fresh snowfall – which often offered a brief reprieve from the shelling and snipers[22] – several young friends take to the streets with their skis. Later, there is a mock-Olympic ceremony: *The winner will receive a kilo of powdered milk. The runner-up will receive some used feta cheese. And where is the third one?* One of the others answers, *Oh, he got killed.* This is juxtaposed with a scene showing one of the actors who has just pulled a bullet from his right shoulder using a set of pliers. Further articulating a sense of cognitive dissonance, Muhamed Kreševljaković, father of Nihad and Sead and then mayor of Sarajevo, is featured in a news clip: "So, something I was once told is now proving to be correct. I was told to count only on the things that are illogical when I once said this city could not be bombed and attacked because it would be illogical. Now everything logical can be thrown away as that for sure is not going to happen."[23] *Do You Remember Sarajevo?* finds fidelity in its fragmentation.

Do You Remember Sarajevo? was also completed the same year Sontag published *Regarding the Pain of Others*, an extended meditation on photographic representations of war. As a rejoinder to her previous work, she asserts that

21. From an introductory address at the 2019 Kairos Prize Awards, which Nihad Kreševljaković was awarded for his longstanding role in theatre programming and cultural projects in Sarajevo. 28 April 2019, Hamburg, Germany.

22. David Rieff, "Midnight in Sarajevo", in *The Atlantic*, April 2000.

23. Nihad Kreševljaković and Sead Kreševljaković, *Do you remember Sarajevo?* film, 2003.

Lawrence Abu Hamdan, ***The All-Hearing***, 2014. Installation view at the 33rd Ljubljana Biennial of Graphic Arts, 2019.

taught him utterance."

MUJO IS LOOKING FOR HIS UNIT'S POSTS ON TREBEVIĆ MOUNTAIN AND HE RUNS INTO A BATTALION OF SERBIAN SOLDIERS.

THEY ASK HIM: *DO YOU KNOW WHO WE ARE?*

AND MUJO REPLIES: *GOD WILLING AND INSHA'ALLAH – YOU ARE CANDID CAMERA.*

there can be no "ecology of images" properly tempered to a (presumed) ethical consumption, but laments the proliferation and ambivalence of journalistic, broadcast, and advertising media for dulling moral and political sensibilities. Sontag wants that a photographic image (with an emphasis on the graphic) should have the power to incite individuals to action – especially those of us who "can't understand, can't imagine."[24] Though intertwined at particular points in their making, *Remember* and *Regarding* suggest two very different politics of the image that mobilise through divergent temporalities, imaginaries, affects, and collectivities. The failures, protraction, and intransigence of the one forced the other. In contrast to extractive journalistic media that circulated widely and quickly, for money, and with some political intent, the home videos show alternative genealogies of image-making as part of the "reinvention of infrastructures" for surviving the everyday. Its transmissions do the long, slow, recursive work of culture over time. In the tragicomedy of *Waiting for Godot* we can perhaps best see these mutually constituted politics of image-making together.

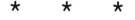

* * *

Hannah Gadsby, who popularised the genre of "Traumedy" with her Netflix stand-up special ***Nanette***, 2018.

Nihad and Sead turned the collection of home videos in their basement into an archive, naming it after their grandfather Hamdija Kreševljaković, the preeminent Bosnian historian who founded the Department of History at Sarajevo University. Hamdija was famous for collecting oral histories to comprise a kind of ethnographic "people's history" of Ottoman and Austro-Hungarian Empires. Reflecting on this continuity, Clarissa Thieme remarked that for Nihad and Sead the video archive "comes from that tradition [but is] translated to their practices and their time." A few years ago, Nihad and Clarissa, together with artist and scholar Jasmina Gavrankapetanović, founded *Izmedzu Nas* (Between Us) as a way of opening the archive to other interested scholars and artists. The project provides a space for the exchange of stories that run counter to public and political discourses about the Bosnian War, and especially offers those who left and those who stayed a way to tell *their* stories. For Thieme, who encountered the *VREMEPLOV* video in the Hamdija Kreševljaković Video Archive, and through a longstanding friendship with the brothers, the laughter in the video – so effervescent, so effecting – provided a point of access, some sense of things beyond sensationalised news coverage and dramatic tropes through which the war was so often narrated. It gave a glimpse of what life was like inside domestic spaces during the siege, and how intimacy was transformed. "Humour opens a space of reflection to take a step aside, to look from a different angle. It opens up to others, it relates."[25]

Laughter here is a mode of communicative vectoring distinct from, but not unlike, translation. Sociologist Norbert Elias pointed to its embodied and transversal aspects: "We know that laughter involves changes at various levels in the person who laughs. There are changes, to mention some, in the blood circulation and the intestines, changes of feeling, of the awareness of others and ourselves, and, of course, changes in our respiration and our face. One can say that the whole organism is involved when a person laughs and that changes

24. Susan Sontag, *Regarding the Pain of Others* (New York: Picador, 2003), p. 98.

25. From an interview with Clarissa Thieme, 14 May 2019, Berlin, Germany.

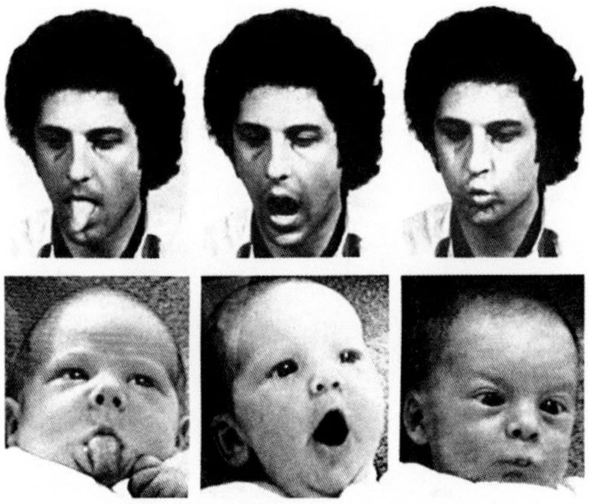

Mirror neurons. Sample photographs taken from videos of infants imitating an adult experimenter.

Intervention in public space at the Skenderija Bridge, Sarajevo. Šejla Kamerić, Naida Begeta and Enes Huseinčehajić, ***Do you remember Sarajevo?***, 2002.

of different parts and at different levels form an ensemble."[26] This *ensemble* is a kind of disjunctive togetherness across scales – riffing and vibrating through bodies, oxygenating the organs, exciting endorphins, stimulating mirror neurons, communicating, connecting – to animate the whole social body. Elias' is a niche theory of laughter, apart from those that many political theorists have offered, which tend to accentuate its effects as a technology of social dominance, or as something that moves us toward behavioural conformity.[27] To be sure, humour is a privilege afforded unequally and unpredictably by some.[28] It also opens up just as often as it closes down. Though at best it may have the capacity to speak truth to power, in its everyday expressions it is more likely to offer a fresh reveal of structures of social difference; by which we differently suffer the (often accidental) comedic candour of others as a series of minor assaults.[29]

But as Elias suggests, though it is always agnostic to its moral content, laughter's properties of embodiment, cohesion, and distribution have the capacity to dispel the tension it is not possible for a body to hold.[30] So-called "gallows humour", dark humour, or what André Breton called *humour noir*, often works this way. It moves in feral forms through affects and aesthetic expressions, and maintains what some have said are its "critical, cohesive, and coping functions."[31] It can play offense (see Monty Python's "The Funniest Joke in the World" sketch) or defence (Hannah Arendt's contentious reading of the Kafkaesque into the figure of Adolf Eichmann). And as a sister of satire, it offers an important caveat to an intellectual genealogy of humour that has located its (hopes for) political agency in discursivity more than bare life itself. As Nihad offered in a recent article, "Humour was without a doubt an important survival tool under the extreme conditions of the Sarajevo siege, and an important means in the defense of citizens of Sarajevo. It was nothing less than a realistic indicator that there was still hope."[32] In certain contexts, the biopolitical stakes of humour come

26. Norbert Elias, "Essay on Laughter" in special issue of *Critical Inquiry: Comedy has Issues* 43:2 (Winter 2017), Lauren Berlant and Sianne Ngai, eds., p. 301.

27. In laughter Thomas Hobbes identified a capacity for social ruin, the "brutishness" of life on full display; to be laughed at – in a moment of "sudden glory" for a social opponent – elicited more shame, more risk, more fear; Henri Bergson understood laughter as "… something mechanical encrusted upon the living."

28. This is particularly true in the historical narrative presented here, which likely skews radically differently through gender, urban / rural, political, and religious difference.

29. Claudia Rankine's *Citizen* shows the brutality of being candid, and the quick deflation of a humorous remark in intimate spaces of friendship structured by racial difference. As she describes in conversation with Lauren Berlant, "Everyone is having a good time together – doing what they do, buying what they can afford, going where they go – until they are not. The break in the encounter wouldn't wound without the presumed intimacy and the good times." *Bomb Magazine*, 1 October 2014.

30. "Traumedy" is a recently coined term (an update to "tragicomic") used to describe a genre of comedic performance that explores tension as a medium of comedic pleasure and personal pain. See stand-up sets *Nanette* by Hannah Gadsby and *Boyish Girl Interrupted* by Tig Notaro.

31. John Morreall, "Humor in the Holocaust: Its Critical, Cohesive, and Coping functions." Paper presented at the Annual Scholars' Conference on the Holocaust, 1997.

32. Nihad Kreševljaković, "Humor under siege: Mujo, don't jump around, you'll get hungry", in *Al Jazeera Balkans*, 22 November 2015.

TOWARDS THE END OF THE WAR, THERE WAS A JOKE ABOUT MUJO AND SULJO, WITH ONE OF THEM SPENDING THE WAR ABROAD AS A REFUGEE, AND THE OTHER ONE SPENDING THE WAR UNDER SIEGE.

BOTH EXHAUSTED BY THEIR EXPERIENCES, THEY DECIDE TO TAKE THE TUNNEL. ONE WANTS TO RETURN TO SARAJEVO, AND THE OTHER WANTS TO ESCAPE FROM IT.

THEY MEET EXACTLY IN THE MIDDLE OF THE TUNNEL AND SHOUT AT THE SAME TIME: *WHERE THE F**K ARE YOU GOING!*

*
Nihad Kreševljaković, "Humor under siege: Mujo, don't jump around, you'll get hungry," in *Al Jazeera Balkans*, 22 November 2015.

into stark relief. Jokes become tools in the art of living, and camcorders weapons of survival, working together to intervene in representations of the graphic dimensions of war; or figuring through the prolongation of a glitch.

Monty Python, ***The Funniest Joke in the World***, 1969.

PAVLIHA

Pavliha is Slovenian folk figure, known as a joker, a funny and roguish person. A humble folk hero, Pavliha is a cunning, wise-fool who seems to always disrupt the social order as he pursues an endless series of misadventures. He is seen as the Slovenian equivalent to characters such as Pulcinella (Italy), Kasperl (Germany), Punch (U.K.), and Petrushka (Russia). The figure of the Pavliha was instrumentalised in various forms of political and popular media throughout the 19th-century. The writer and editor Fran Levstik (1831–1887) published the influential satirical journal *Pavliha* beginning in 1870. This featured political commentary, humorous columnists, and an abundance of caricatures that over time targeted Western capitalist countries (with issues such as the question of the borders between Italy and Austria) and other domestic and foreign enemies (fascists, Nazis, imperialists, war criminals, traitors, reactionaries, and church dignitaries).

Additionally, the ethnologist Dr. Niko Kuret helped popularise Pavliha in Slovenian

puppet theatre between the World Wars. The puppeteer Jože Pengov voiced and animated the Pavliha character in skits on Radio Ljubljana and in theatres. He later founded the Ljubljana Puppet Theatre, bringing Pavliha to wider audiences. The work of these two men was part of the larger *Sokol* (Falcon) puppetry movement, prominent throughout Central and Eastern Europe during this interim period. Developing from the traveling puppet shows and performances in small, makeshift "family theatres" during the 19th-century, the Sokol movement saw the emergence of new institutions, including associations, trade schools, and puppet theatres, that merged folk performance and sculptural traditions with new avant-garde aesthetics and political content.

BETWEEN THREE REVOLUTIONS

NOTES ON THE HISTORY OF IRANIAN POLITICAL SATIRE

MOHAMMAD SALEMY

The history of socio-ethical satire in Iran prior to the Constitutional Revolution of 1905 stretches back to medieval times, and includes figures like Obeid Zakani, Hafiz, Saadi, and Baba Tahir. Far from assimilating Western genres, Persian literary satire had its own theories, which divided the discourse into the categories of MOTAYEBEH (مطایبه), meant as light and pleasant jokes, HAJ'V (هجو), the opposite of praise, and HA Z'L (هزل) criticism that contains sexually explicit content. Throughout this history, the razor-sharp edge of Persian satire was aimed mostly at the Royal Court and other wealthy people for their excesses, and the clergy for their hypocrisies in enforcing Islamic morality. During the reign of the Pahlavis, satire turned to politics; as a result of censorship, satirists took to criticising the regime by poking fun at Iran's hegemonic allies like the U.K. and the U.S. As a result of the 1979 Islamic Revolution led by Ayatollah Khomeini, political satire returned to an age-old criticism of Islamic morality while keeping its anti-imperialist impulses. This new but short-lived political satire, represented mostly in the Marxist weekly satirical paper *Ahanger* (آهنگر), not only criticised the revolutionary state's gradual attempt at imposing an Islamic moral code on society, but also exaggerated the still-illegal actions of pro-Khomeini organisations and individuals. This produced what I call Speculative Political Satire. It painted a picture of a future Iran under the total control of Islamists, and used this speculation as a wake-up call to secular Iranians who weren't sure which way the revolution was heading. Forty years later, this rich historical legacy has now fallen on the shoulders of a younger generation of political satirists using new mediums like Twitter, texts, and Instagram memes in the context of global social media. They are providing a social critique of Iranian societies, both at home and amongst the diaspora, while maintaining their focus on Islamism and other forms of moralism and hypocrisy, which still dominate public political discourse in Iran.

Published a few months before the 1953 coup that deposed the democratically elected Prime Minister Mossadegh, the cartoon depicts Mohammad Reza Pahlavi alongside the King of Iran and Queen Soraya, embodied as cats. The King eats from the state funds, (which belong to the people), while the Prime Minister tries to shoo him away. The old man in the background represents the Iranian people.

The caption reads: "Are you really expecting to eat while I pretend I am the cat? Meow, meow, meow."

Above the image: "Retired professionals will be reinvited to work." The Constitutional Angel to the Minister: "Swear to god I was retired during the last government." (Referring to the 1953 coup.)

The original logo for *Ahangar Satirical Weekly* (in black) as it appeared in its first issue, printed over the logo (in red) of an earlier paper called *Chalangar*, published in the late 1940s and early 1950s by Mohammad Ali Afrashteh (pictured), a member of the Iranian Communist (*Toudeh*) Party. This act, protested immediately by the Party, was meant to suggest a historical continuity between the two papers in terms of form and content.

The original slogan of *Chalangar*, written above the red star, reads: "Be broken: the pen and the hand, which disobeys from serving the needy."

The cartoon speculates a possible sexual segregation of television in the Islamic Republic. It depicts Sadegh Ghotbzadehm, the first director of the Iranian National Radio and Television Broadcasting Company after the revolution. On the right, the masculine-looking female television announcer who, it is suggested, was hired because of her "bad looks" (so as to not sexually provoke the male viewers), is covered in Islamic headdress.

The caption reads: "The gender segregated television."

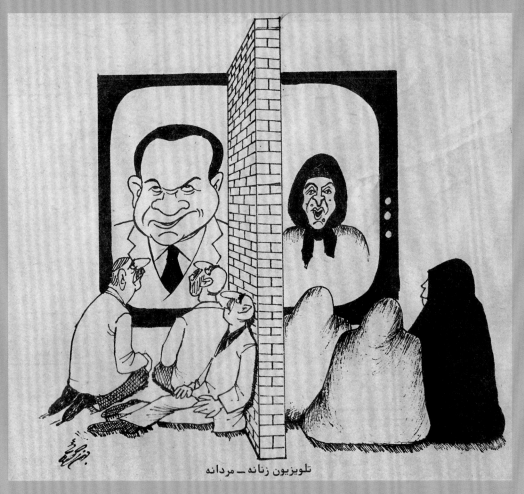

۱۲ صفحه

۲۰ ریال

آهنگر

سال اول شماره ۱۳ سه‌شنبه ۲۶ تیر ۱۳۵۸

سکوت‌انقلابی!

علا مه‌درگزینی

"خموشی پاسبان اهل راز است
ازو کبک ایمن‌ازچنگال‌بازاست"
گر آگه باشی از قدر خموشی
نخواهی‌رفت دنبال چموشی!
خموشی با کمی غسل و طهارت
مساویست باصدارت با وزارت
بیا بنشین توای جانانه فرزند
دراین‌معناتوراپندی‌دهم‌چند
اگر بینی وزیری در نهانی
بود با خارجی اندر تبانی
مدارک در سفارت هرچه موجود
بنا گه میشود معدوم و مفقود
توهم‌خود را بزن بر پرده پوشی
خموشی‌پیشه‌کن‌جانا ، خموشی
وگر بینی که دزد نفتخواره
دوصد پیمان سرّی با تو داره
بدستاویز آن پیمان بی پا
برد داروندارت را به‌یغما
چو می‌بینی وزیری با سماجت
ازآن‌پیمان‌نماید رفع حاجت!
بزن‌خودرابه‌خواب ومثل‌خرگوش
بشین‌درگوشه‌ای‌آرام‌وخاموش
اگر بینی زمام و سرنوشتت
تمام سرنوشت خوب و زشتت
بود اندر کف افراد مخفی
مکن قرقر بسان پنکه سقفی !
بگو قربان گوارا بادتان ، نوش
دوچشمت‌رابهم‌بگذاروخاموش!
وگر بینی که در ارتش خبرهاست
وآن‌دعوا سر پوستین ملاست

The cartoon depicts the state of the revolution and the transitional government ministers including Prime Minister Bazargan, Minister of Culture Minachi, and Minister of Labour Forouhar (later murdered by rouge elements of the information ministry in 1998). While it is the heavyweight of Islamic fundamentalism (depicted by the traditional-looking fat man) that is sinking the ship of the revolution, the State throws freedom of press (the woman in a white dress), workers, and ethnic minorities into the sea to reduce the weight of the vessel.

A nurse from the maternity ward presents a newborn to her father.

The caption reads: “Congratulations, your baby is a girl.”

This cartoon deals with the tricks used on the educated Iranian middle class by the post-revolutionary state media to convince them to participate in the 1979 referendum and vote yes for the Islamic Republic system.

The caption reads from top: "Before the referendum, during the referendum, after the referendum."

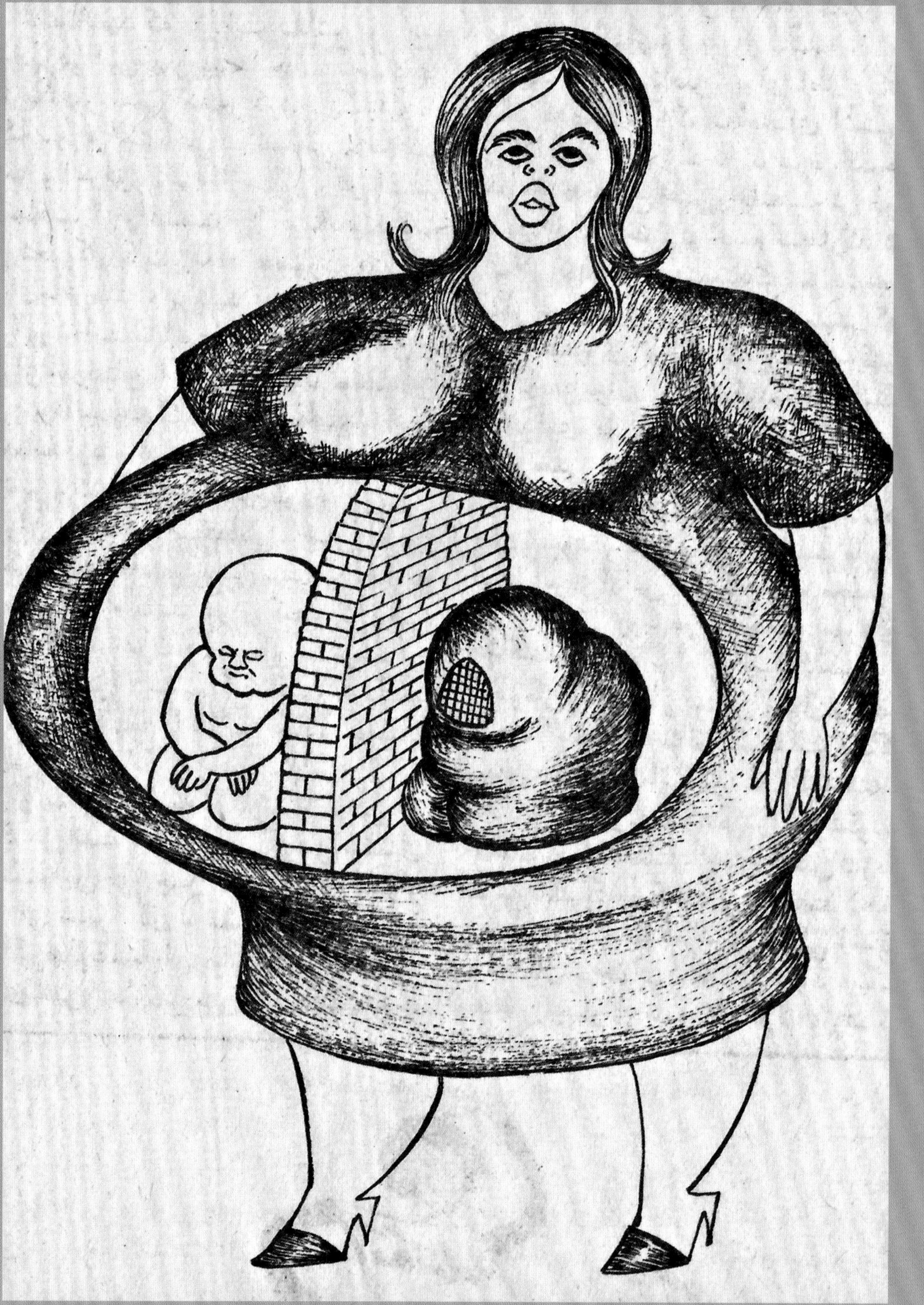

This future-oriented cartoon points to the real possibility of sexual segregation for unborn children in an Islamic Iran.

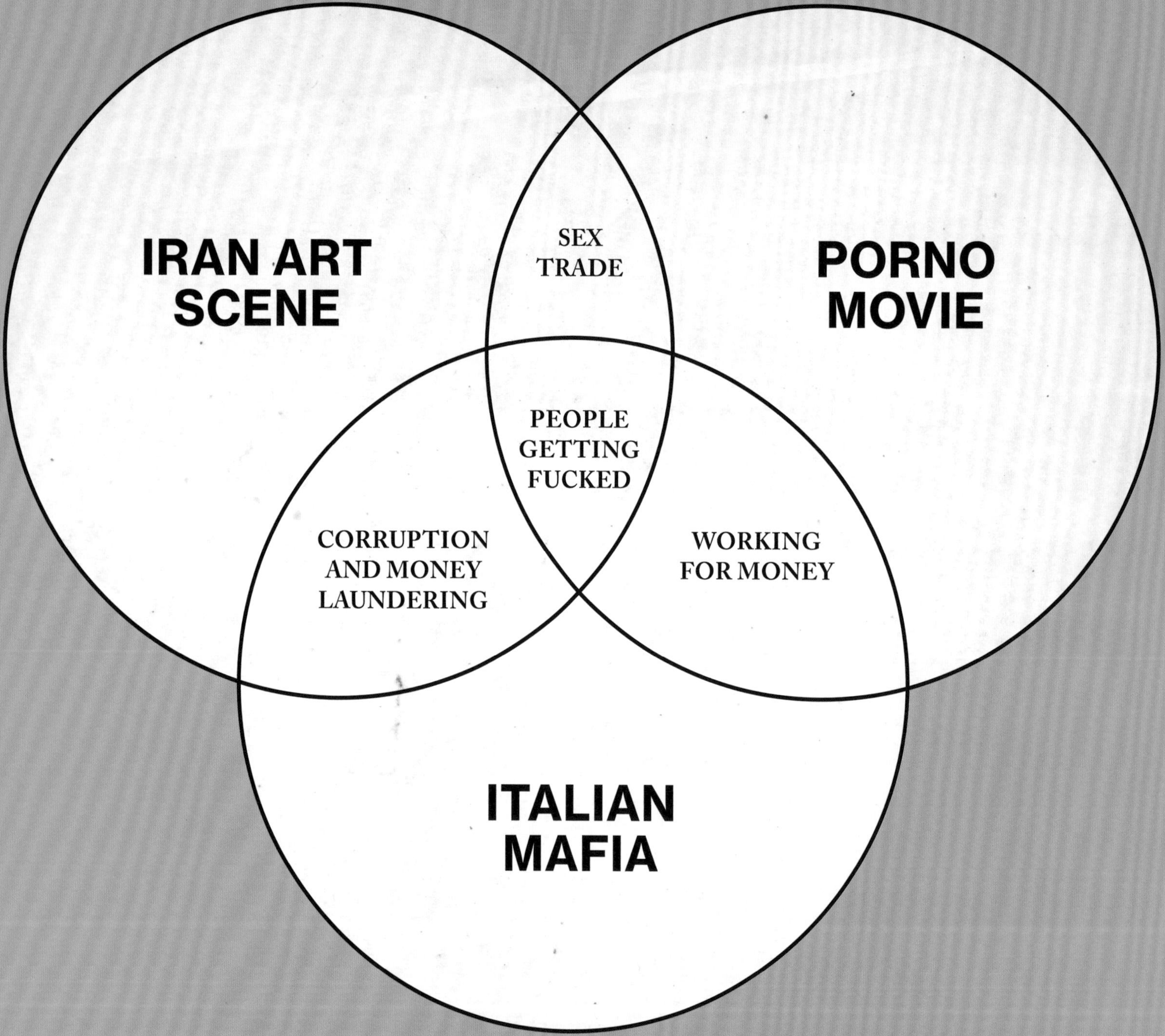

The popular Instagram account "iran_art_meme" produces humorous daily memes about the affairs of the tight-knit contemporary art scene in Iran, often blending sharp social criticism with poignant graphics.

تاریخ ایران
خوشو جر میده که
به ایرانی درس بده
ایرانی

Produced by Kasra Rahmanian, a Milan-based young queer Iranian artist, this Instagram meme account focuses on contradictions within Iranian culture as they pertain to politics de jure, and uses humour to advocate LGBT rights.

The caption reads: (left) “Iranian history killing itself to teach a lesson to Iranians.” (right) “Iranians.”

Taken from blogs, Facebook, and Instagram, the account focuses exclusively on visual phenomena coming from the Islamic Republic of Iran in its fourth decade of existence, exposing the bizarre and unexplainable manifestations that result from the inevitable blend of modern life, technology, and the religious state.

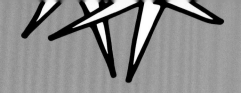

The image points to the legal inequality between men and women built into Islamic law.

— من این حرفها سرم نمیشه ، تو قباله‌ازدواجتون ننوشته که شما میتونین
پهلوی هم بخوابین . . .

A member of the Revolutionary Guard with a gun in his hand, separating a couple in bed.

The caption reads: "I'm not convinced; there is nothing in your marriage contract about sleeping next to each other."

TAKING CARE OF YOURSELF IS DETRIMENTAL TO YOUR HEALTH

ALENKA PIRMAN & KULA

We, Slovenes, are a sporting nation and it had been long believed that half of health – both physical and mental – stems from exercise. Especially so if it takes place outdoors, in nature. However, the latest scientific findings reveal the opposite: not only is exercise not beneficial, it is even harmful! Due to a particular physical characteristic of Slovenes, i.e, for the above-average volume and exceptional vital capacity of our lungs, exercise turns out to be harmful, and physical activity results in poisoning ourselves. Thus taking care of ourselves, as we knew it, is actually detrimental to our health!

THE VITAL CAPACITY OF OUR LUNGS IS ONE OF THE HIGHEST IN EUROPE!

A long-term study carried out by the Domestic Research Institute (*Inštitut za domače raziskave*, hereafter referred to as the DRI) and the Biopolitical Theory and Practice Division of the Slovene Ethnological and Anthropological Association KULA (*Sekcija za biopolitično teorijo in prakso Slovenskega etnološkega in antropološkega združenja KULA*, hereafter referred to as BPaTaPD), whose mission is to monitor and study the evolution, anatomy, and physiology of the lungs of Slovenes, has uncovered a number of significant facts. The most noteworthy thereof are the following: In the period 1977–1997 the average lung volume increased by 9.7%, and by a further 11.2% in the years 1997–2017 (see diagram at the bottom of following page). Similar changes are also observable with regard to lung strength, i.e, the vital capacity of Slovene lungs, which increased from 3.8 litres four decades ago to 5.1 litres by the end of the 1990s, and currently amounts to 6.0 litres. Comparing the results of our studies with those obtained by researchers abroad reveals stagnation in the development of the lungs of almost all other Europeans, which raises the question of why the situation is so very different for Slovenes.

DETRIMENTAL EFFECTS OF PHYSICAL ACTIVITY – EVEN CHILDREN ARE AT RISK!

When the data was contextualised, the immense popularity and frequency of outdoor recreational activities stood out. Even the youngest are encouraged to exercise: we try to get preschoolers accustomed to physical activity. In primary schools, a mandatory daily hour of physical education is being introduced; children participate in mass recreation events, and a variety of after-school activities are offered. Furthermore, different forms of aerobic exercise predominate, e.g, walking, running, cycling, mountaineering, swimming, and cross-country skiing. These are forms of exercise that have been shown to strengthen the respiratory system.

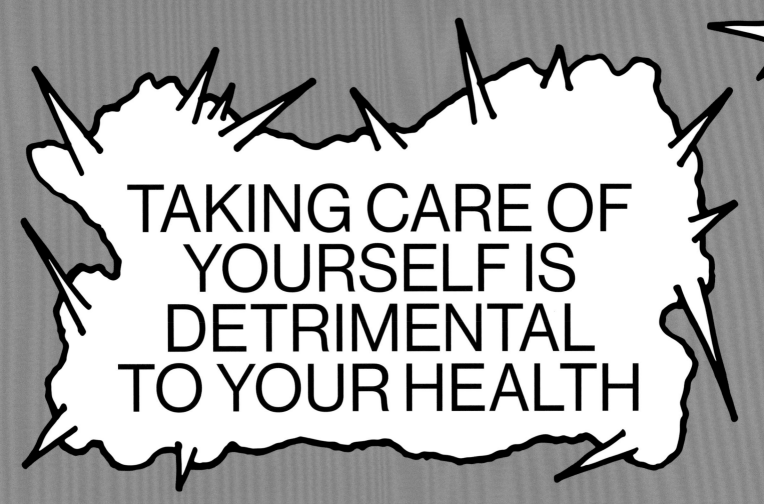

RESEARCH REVEALS: WE ARE EXPOSED TO ENORMOUS RISK AND DANGER!

So what exactly is the problem? Why would something hitherto deemed to be beneficial be actually harmful? Why have these anatomical and physiological gains turned out to be a Pyrrhic victory for us? Twenty years ago, the idea that strengthening the lungs could produce an anomaly seemed like an odd, even ridiculous, notion. Today, however, it is becoming apparent that this idea, which in the past only the most cynical a person could have dreamt up, is unfortunately true.

Due to a variety of factors whose effects on the body and spirit are only now being discovered, large and powerful lungs pose an enormous risk and danger – especially for those who are physically active outdoors on a regular basis. As is well known, air in Slovenia, especially in the vicinity of major cities and in valleys and basins, is heavily polluted. Higher levels of PM10 and z2.5 particles, which pass through the alveoli of the lungs and into the bloodstream, and thus throughout the body, are being recorded on a regular basis. It has been proven that such particles increase the mortality rate through increasing the likelihood of respiratory and cardiovascular diseases. They are particularly dangerous when they contain heavy metals, which intensify inflammations, increase the degree of tissue death, have negative consequences for the functioning of the brain and nervous system, and influence the onset of Parkinson's and Alzheimer's diseases, etc.

The same holds true of nitrogen dioxide, carbon monoxide, sulfur dioxide, and benzene. Benzene is especially dangerous. According to the IARC, it is classified as a Group 1 carcinogen (the link is most evident with regard to leukemia and other forms of blood cancer). Yet awareness of the hazard posed by this substance has not yet been cultivated in the general public. In Slovenia, measurement of the content of benzene in the atmosphere has only recently commenced. The situation is similar for airborne micro- and nanoplastics, whose negative effects we can only guess at.

Furthermore, it has been hypothesised that the relaxation and enthusiasm one experiences during physical activity are a consequence of the compound

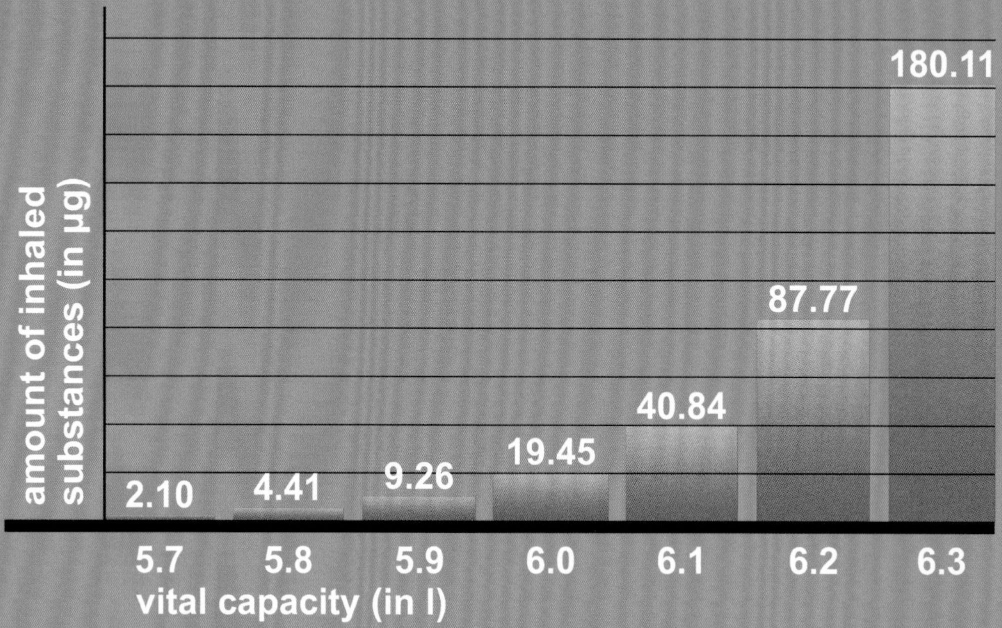

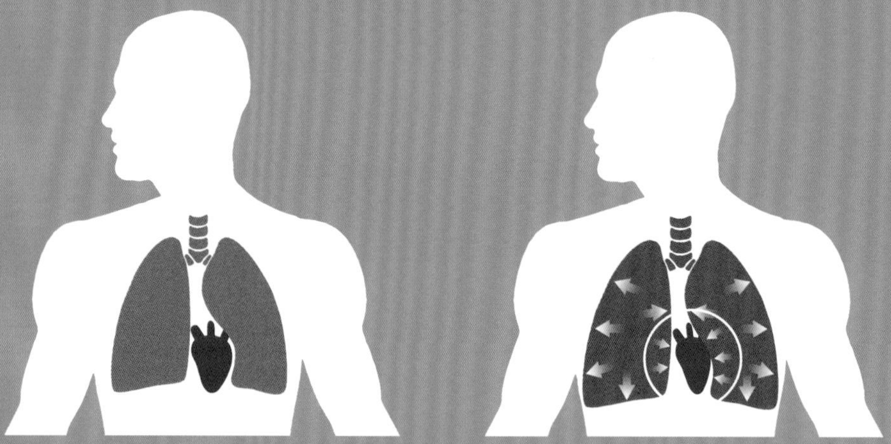

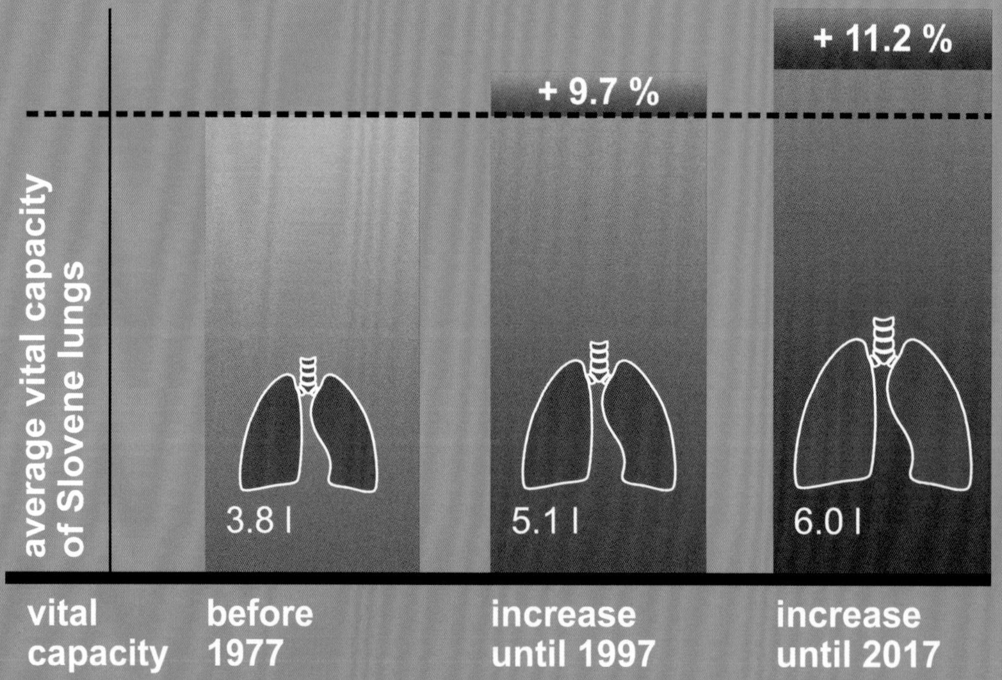

6-monoacetylmorphine, which forms in the brain in a way that is not yet understood. Perhaps the reason for the formation of this dangerous compound is the extraordinary ability of Slovenes to inhale elements found in the air. Thus, the popular notion that Slovenes are obsessed with recreational activity is well explained and justified.

In short, based on measurements, we at BPaTaPD have determined that during physical exercise Slovenes breathe into their over-developed, almost superhumanly large and well-functioning lungs and therefore take vast amounts of various pollutants into their bodies. Namely, it can be noted that by strengthening the lungs and increasing the frequency of hyperpnoea, i.e, the phases of prolonged breathing effort – as can be seen in, for example, aerobic forms of exercise – the absorption of gases and particulates found in the air increases exponentially!

THE "SMALL HEARTS" OF SLOVENES EXPLAINED!

The first anomalies have already appeared. Preliminary measurements of the organs most active in physical exertion reveal an unusual effect on the heart. Also in this regard new questions have arisen whose answers require further research, but it would seem that lung growth has been too rapid for the growth of the thorax and ribs. This disproportionality has created a real logjam in the chest and severely limited the space available for heart function and growth. The result is a deformation of the heart, which is becoming ever smaller, especially among enthusiastic athletes and Slovenes in general. At the same time, the possibility of serious heart failure or even an acute myocardial infarction (which has been witnessed in recent years at several mass recreational sporting events) is increasing. It is certain that due to the higher percentage of athletes among Slovenes the health budget is suffering, a situation that will only be exacerbated in the future. Moreover, for now it is impossible to imagine what the consequences will be for each individual, and not least the whole nation, if we continue to live in the manner that we have thus far, and further encourage our children, who are already too active, to pursue physical activity.

LET'S TAKE ACTION NOW!

In order to prevent the worst-case scenario, we must act now. Everyone is responsible for his or her own health. At this time, the BPaTaPD can do nothing else but invite responsible and dedicated individuals to limit their recreational activities, although we are aware that the solutions must also be systemic. Therefore, the BPaTaPD is formulating a set of proposals that we will shortly submit to the Ministry of Health

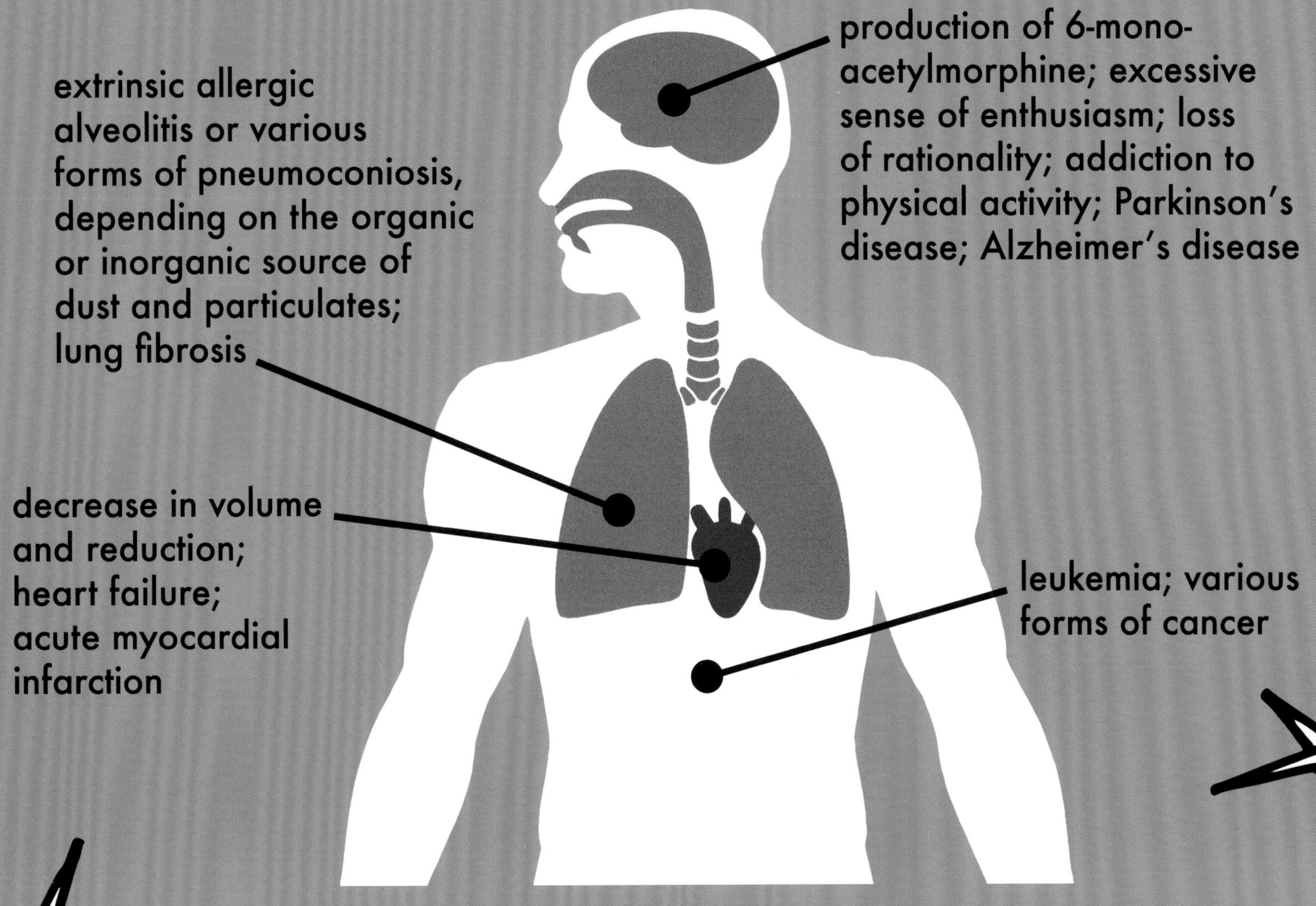

and the Ministry of Education, Science, and Sport. These will be related to higher taxes on sports equipment (running shoes, bicycles, etc.), the introduction of a duty on recreational activities, the replacement of physical education in primary and secondary schools with lessons on the culture of stillness, and an increase in state subsidies in the field of sitting aids, as well as tax cuts for businesses that discourage and limit the movement of their employees.
But, as we know all too well, bureaucratic mills are far too slow to do their job properly and promptly. The only way to act in the current situation is to reduce the time we spend exercising / on recreational activities without delay, if we cannot completely renounce it. Every ending is difficult, but we must try.

Those who have given stillness a chance have learnt to love it. In order to be still, most effectively, one needs a chair or even an armchair in which one fits comfortably, and a good book, movie, or computer game. In such manner, after a long and exhausting day of work, we will exercise our minds without burdening the respiratory and cardiovascular system.
By reducing the number of hours spent on a running track or bicycle we will at least slightly reduce our biological intake of toxic airborne substances, and as well retard, if not redirect, the development of Slovene lungs. In order to raise public awareness and promote stillness, we are organising the first traditional Sit-down for a Good Purpose Festival, which means sitting for those who can't (more information to come soon). In truth, everyone is responsible for his or her own health. It is only by properly caring for ourselves that we can ensure the welfare everyone!

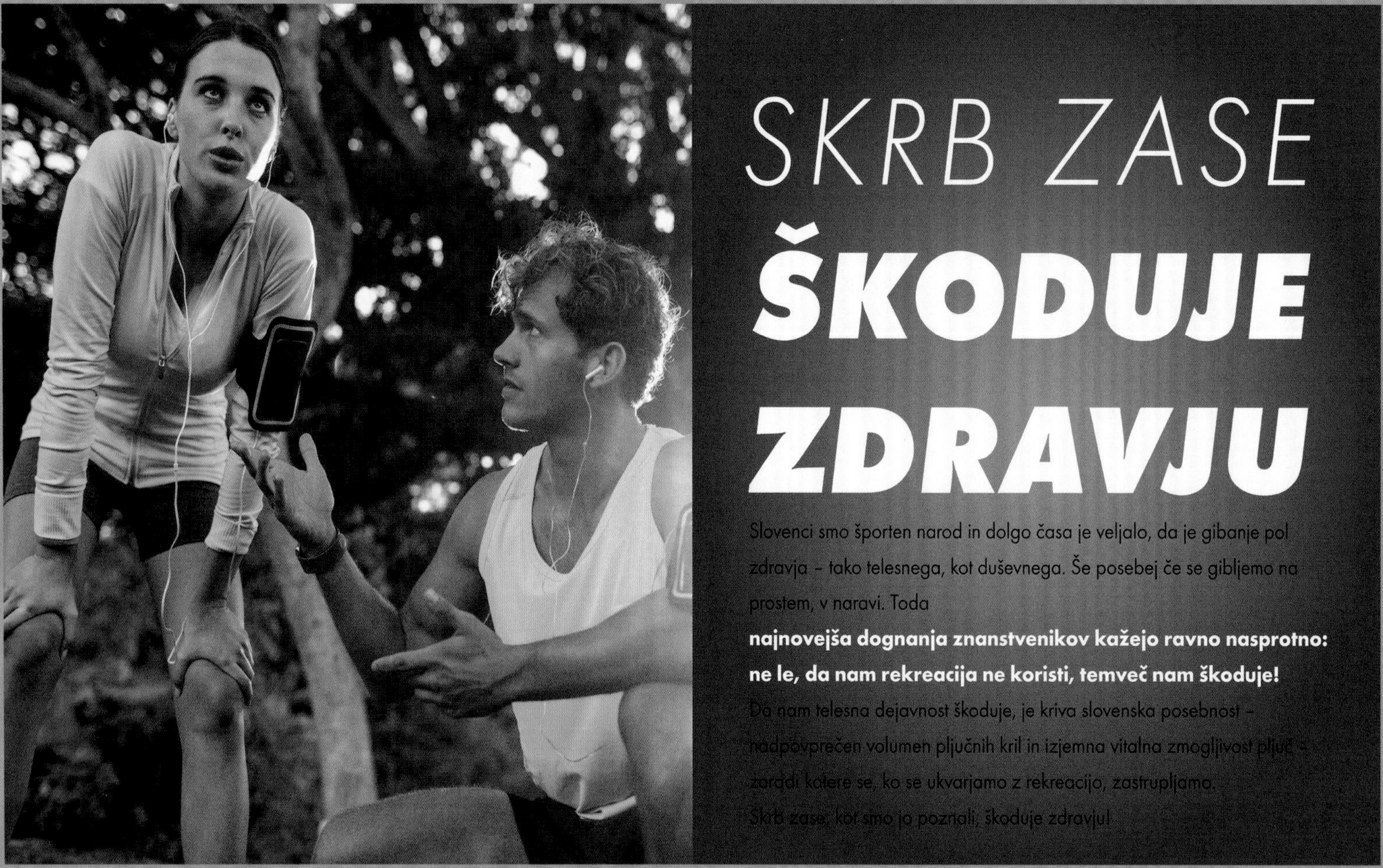

SKRB ZASE
ŠKODUJE
ZDRAVJU
Slovenci smo športen narod in dolgo časa je veljalo, da je gibanje pol zdravja – tako telesnega, kot duševnega. Še posebej če se gibljemo na prostem, v naravi. Toda
najnovejša dognanja znanstvenikov kažejo ravno nasprotno: ne le, da nam rekreacija ne koristi, temveč nam škoduje!
Da nam telesna dejavnost škoduje, je kriva slovenska posebnost – nadpovprečen volumen pljučnih kril in izjemna vitalna zmogljivost pljuč – zaradi katere se, ko se ukvarjamo z rekreacijo, zastrupljamo.
Skrb zase, kot smo jo poznali, škoduje zdravju!

Alenka Pirman & KULA (Slovenian Ethnological and Anthropological Association), ***Taking Care of Yourself is Detrimental to Your Health. A campaign***, 2019. Design and diagrams by Tomaž Perme.

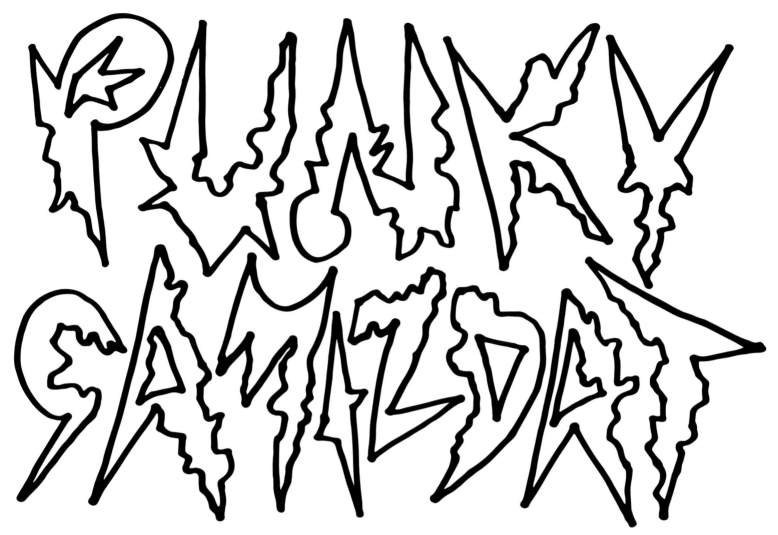

PUNKY SAMIZDAT

DAVID CROWLEY

'IDIOTS JUST LIKE US'

Brygada Kryzys, LP, live recording, 1982.

Punk arrived in fits and starts in Eastern Europe in the late 1970s. In some places, it sprouted from little more than a misheard rumour or an accidental encounter on the airwaves. In Leningrad, Yevgeny Yufit, later known for his lickerish Necrorealist films, recalled, "The only source of music information was a shortwave radio that I would use to listen to the BBC. In 1977 I heard a new group – the Sex Pistols – and I remember telling Svin (Andrei Panov) 'In England there are idiots just like us!'[1] Michael Kobs of the East German band Planlos (meaning No Plan or Aimless) also recalls tuning into the BBC's World Service: "I listened to western radio in the 70s – mainly John Peel's show. That was a new musical world. At some point I got a Clash poster, don't remember where from. Only then did I see pictures depicting punk."[2] Sometimes, proto-punks in Eastern Europe pieced together their understanding from hatchet jobs in the official press. Typically, punk was presented as a symptom of the degeneracy of "the rotting West" in state media.[3] But Eastern European readers living under communist rule were well-versed in reading "against the grain", i.e, reversing the claims of state propaganda or, as we'll see, taking reports at their word. Robert Brylewski, founder of Kryzys, an early punk rock outfit in Poland, recalled reading a report mocking British punks in a Warsaw daily. He decided

1. Yevgeny in *What About Tomorrow? An Oral History of Russian Punk* (Portland, Oregon: Microcosm Publishing) forthcoming.

2. Michael "Pankow" Boehlke, interview by Bodo Mrozek, *OstPunk!: too much future : Punk in der DDR 1979–1989*, ed. Michael Boehlke (Berlin: Künstlerhaus Bethanien, 2005), p. 48.

3. http://www.vladimir-kozlov.com/Eng/Punk.html. Accessed 15 February 2019.

The Raincoats, 1979.

Einstürzende Neubauten, 1985.

Ella Kruglyanskaya, ***The Black Leather Jacket*** for a charity auction held by Barneys and Christie's, 2016.

to adopt the chief object of ridicule – the safety pin worn as jewellery – and went out into the city wearing fifteen of them. Encountering a man in a trench coat, the tell-tale uniform of the *ubek* (secret policeman), he imagined his own imminent arrest, only to find that his observer pulled open his collar to reveal his own collection of punk pins.[4]

Originating in the West, punk was always a patchy signal in the Eastern Bloc and Yugoslavia. Some settings had better reception than others: the young had more opportunities to connect in Yugoslavia and Poland than the more closed worlds of Czechoslovakia and the Soviet Union. The London post-punk feminist group The Raincoats played an early gig in Warsaw in 1978, for instance. And when punk gestures were made, they were always acts of adaption in which sounds, images, and fashions with alien origins were given "local" forms. Incomplete knowledge stimulated a kind of heightened imagination too. After all, for citizens of the Eastern Bloc, punk and later new wave belonged to what Andrei Yurchak has called an "*imaginary* west … that [for Soviet citizens] was simultaneously knowable and unobtainable, tangible and abstract, mundane and exotic."[5] Reviewing the first wave of industrial bands in East Germany in 1985, Christoph Tannert, a young promoter and musician, claimed that having never seen groups from the West like Einstürzende Neubauten and Test Department perform "saved" his compatriots from "epigonism" and the "rust" of copying the "old metalworkers".[6]

Soviet proto-punks, more isolated than their Polish, East German, and Yugoslav counterparts, had little to go on and all the more to fill in. They seemed more inclined to embrace punk as an attitude. Ivan Gololobov writes:

4. This account is given by Raymond A. Patton in *Punk Crisis: The Global Punk Rock Revolution* (Oxford: Oxford University Press, 2018), p. 48.

5. Alexei Yurchak, *Everything Was Forever, Until it Was No More. The Last Soviet Generation* (Princeton and Oxford: Princeton University Press, 2006), p. 159.

6. Tannert writing under the pseudonym Britta Lagerfeldt, "Coswig 1985" in David Crowley and Daniel Muzyczuk, eds., *Notes from the Underground: Art and Alternative Music in Eastern Europe, 1968–1994* (Łódź: Muzeum Sztuki, 2016), p. 388.

> *... the very late 1970s saw the first few signs of a new anti-aesthetics emerging among scattered handfuls of young people in Moscow and Leningrad. They could not be categorised as the by-now familiar* bitniki, stilyagi, *or Soviet hippies, and did not share their admiration for Western culture. They wore their hair short and preferred Soviet-brand clothes, which they wore proudly, in often unusual ways: a stained old jacket with a tie on a bare chest; a naval shirt with smart trousers a few sizes too small; a long coat with white pumps and a ladies' fancy scarf. Some wore badges, various self-made accessories, safety pins or key rings. The common denominator among such absurd variety was that, in the eyes of the average citizen, they looked like idiots and their behaviour tended to match their clown-like dress style. Loud-mouthed, grimacing and awkward-moving, they celebrated all shades of teenage dysfunction. Demonstratively ignoring the concerns and behavioural codes of respectable citizens, these young people seemingly enjoyed being regarded and treated as imbeciles.*[7]

Moscow punks, 1988.

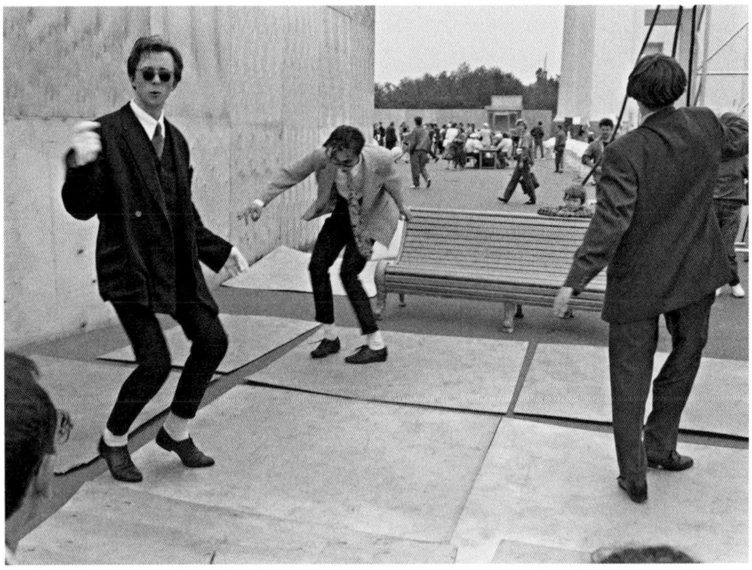

Stilyagi, Moscow mods of the late 1950s dancing the Twist.

The Mukhomor (Toadstool) Group of youthful artists in the late 1970s, for instance, might be understood as proto-punks in this way.[8] They started their activities – actions, amateurish paintings, and improvised sound collages – in the orbit of non-conformist artists Andrei Monastyrsky and Ilya Kabakov, but quickly rejected the subtle lyricism of Moscow Conceptualism in favour of more absurd and even brutal aesthetics that shared much in common with punk. One action, *Raasstrel* (*Execution*, 1979), involved a mock execution of a volunteer drawn from the audience that had gathered in a forest to watch the Mukhomor's artistic performance. Alluding to the Bol'shoj terror (Great Terror), the action disturbed some of the audience, perhaps because of its literalism.[9] Mukhomor's other works included *Zolotoj disk* (*Golden Disk*), a sound collage recorded in 1980–1981, composed "from assorted tape recordings, from Little Richard to Soviet patriotic marches, Vivaldi symphonies to Central Asian folklore, state anthems to recent pop hits, overlaid with their own wild performance

7. Ivan Gololobov, Hilary Pilkington, and Yngvar B. Steinholt, *Punk in Russia: Cultural Mutation from the 'Useless' to the 'Moronic'* (London and New York: Routledge, 2014), p. 23.

8. The Mukhomor group was created in 1978 by Sven Gundlach, Konstantin Zvezdochetov, Alexey Kamensky and Mironenko brothers Vladimir and Sergey and operated for ca. six years.

9. See Matthew Jesse Jackson, *The Experimental Group: Ilya Kabakov, Moscow Conceptualism, Soviet Avantgardes* (Chicago: University of Chicago Press, 2010), pp. 213–214.

Punk Problemi, Vol. 11, No. 10/11, edited by Peter Mlakar, Ljubljana, 1983, RK ZSMS. Cover photograph by Jane Štravs.

of self-composed poems and short stories."[10] Copied on reel-to-reel tapes, it circulated throughout the Soviet Union, becoming an underground "hit", even making money for the group according to one report.[11] The Mukhomor Group also claimed to be The Beatles in a handmade book in 1982. Posing for the camera in the streets, courtyards, and rooftops of Moscow, they created a photo album which starts with the assertion, "We are two Beatles – Kostya and I". This is group member Sven Gundlakh's own description:

> *At the beginning of the book* The Beatles *by The Mukhomor Group there was still some sense of subject, but by the third page until the very end it is filled with photographs of bums dancing and uneven lines of sound composition like "Bdu, bda, bdla", which seem to imitate scat singing.*[12]

Occupying a space between enthusiasm and self-ridicule, *The Beatles* is an example of what Gundlakh called "mental pop art", an attitude in which "philosophy" is expressed in "completely idiotic and banal ideas".[13] And the dissonance and biting humour of the "Golden Disk" was not only a dismissal of the trite and often sentimental culture promoted by the Soviet state, but also of the earnest and highbrow activities of non-conformist artists. With a deadpan taste for imbecility, The Mukhomor Group was one stream of a new wave of punk-like attitudes in Moscow in the early 1980s.

PUNK PROBLEMI

***Novi Punk Val* (*New Punk Wave*)**, 1981.

The responses of the communist authorities to punk groupuscules was far from consistent, even in the same country, and usually veered between suppression and co-option. In Yugoslavia in 1981, a compilation LP was issued under the title *Novi Punk Val 78–80*, and Siouxsie and the Banshees were invited to play by the Student Centre in Ljubljana. And yet this was the same year that the authorities in the Socialist Republic of Slovenia sought to extinguish the subculture by denouncing its "fascist" tendencies. In a campaign known as the Nazi-Punk Affair, an obscure band was prosecuted for racist lyrics, and a wave of arrests and interrogations occupied the police for much of the autumn.[14] Supporting the state, major newspapers denounced punks in hysterical terms, in turn triggering attacks on the streets and expulsions from school. Intellectuals rallied in defence. Three "punk" issues of *Problemi* (*Problems*), an important philosophical journal under the editorship of Mladen Dolar, were published between 1981 and 1983, for instance. *Problemi* identified closely with its subject, adopting the cut-and-paste Xerox aesthetics of fanzines, and reproducing the lyrics of many of the most openly critical bands including Pankrti (Bastards), as well as newspaper reports of punk from around the world, and darkly dystopian comic strips. In the first of these three punk issues, the celebrated neo-Lacanian philosopher Slavoj Žižek supplied an editorial reflecting on punk (written before the Nazi-Punk Affair). He describes punk not as an alien phenomenon imported from the West but as

10. Artemy Troitsky, *Tusovka: Who's Who in New Soviet Rock Culture* (London: Omnibus, 1990), p. 30.
11. See Andrew Solomon, *The Irony Tower. Soviet Artists in the Time of Glasnost* (New York: Knopf, 1991), p. 110.
12. Sven Gundlakh, "APTART. Pictures from an exhibition" in *A-ya* 5 (1983), p. 14.
13. Cited by Jackson, *The Experimental Group*, p. 215.
14. See Jones Irwin and Helena Motoh, *Žižek and His Contemporaries: On the Emergence of the Slovenian Lacan* (London: Bloomsbury, 2014), p. 31.

Messitsch, Nos. 4 (left) and 2 (right), Leipzig, September and July 1990.

a "symptom [that] reveals an intrusion of the suppressed 'truth' of the most calm, most normal everyday life" in Yugoslavia:[15]

> *Punk literally depicts the deprived vastness of the "normal", and already this "liberates": it introduces some alienating distance. This is why the sadomasochism, irrational violence, "anarchy", etc, of punk are so emphasised. Yet punk introduces this distance exactly as it re-enacts these elements, when it "resurfaces" them.*

East Germany (GDR) appears to have been a particularly repressive environment, with the state operating a system of licenses to determine who could play music in public, and running informants to manage the emergent punk scene from within. Following the official line, Stasi files described punks as being "of weak character", "disoriented", easily influenced and shaped by the "Western enemy", and as "degenerate" with a "lack of belief in socialist ideals."[16] Punk seems to have been viewed as more of a threat in the GDR than it was in Poland or Hungary; punk fanzines were a rarity there, for instance. The historian Christian Schmidt has traced the first East German title to a pamphlet by Jörg Löffler, printed in just three copies in Dresden in 1983, and produced on

15. See Slavoj Žižek, "Introduction to Punk Problemi" in David Crowley and Daniel Muzyczuk, eds., *Notes from the Underground: Art and Alternative Music in Eastern Europe, 1968–1994* (Łódź: Muzeum Sztuki, 2016), p. 412.

16. See Juliane Brauer, "Clashes of Emotions: Punk Music, Youth Subculture, and Authority in the GDR (1978–1983)" in *Juvenile Delinquency, Modernity, and the State*, 38:4 (2012), p. 59.

Henryk Gajewski, Polish punk promoter.

a typewriter using carbon copying paper.[17] One of the copies sent to the West was intercepted, and Löffler was held on remand for three months. Another, with the title *Inside*, was printed in 400 copies in Poland. It was confiscated and destroyed by the customs authorities when its editor tried to bring it into East Germany. Schmidt has only been able to identify two other titles produced in the country (*Alösa*, printed by a punk congregation associated with an evangelical East Berlin church as an "information sheet" between 1986–1988, and *Messitsch*, printed in 1987 in a Leipzig darkroom on photographic paper). To avoid the very real risk of being imprisoned for unauthorised publication, East German punk writers had to be satisfied with sending their articles and images to West Germany for publication in fanzines on the other side of the Wall.

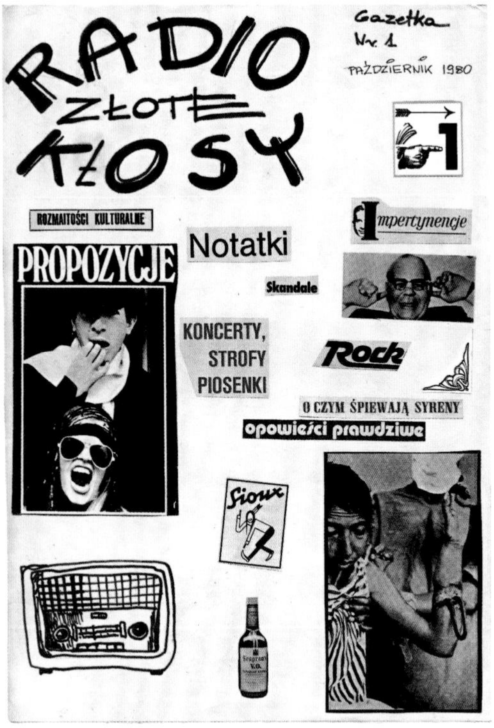

'Ada' Dąbrowska, ***Radio Złote Kłosy***, Warsaw, October 1980.

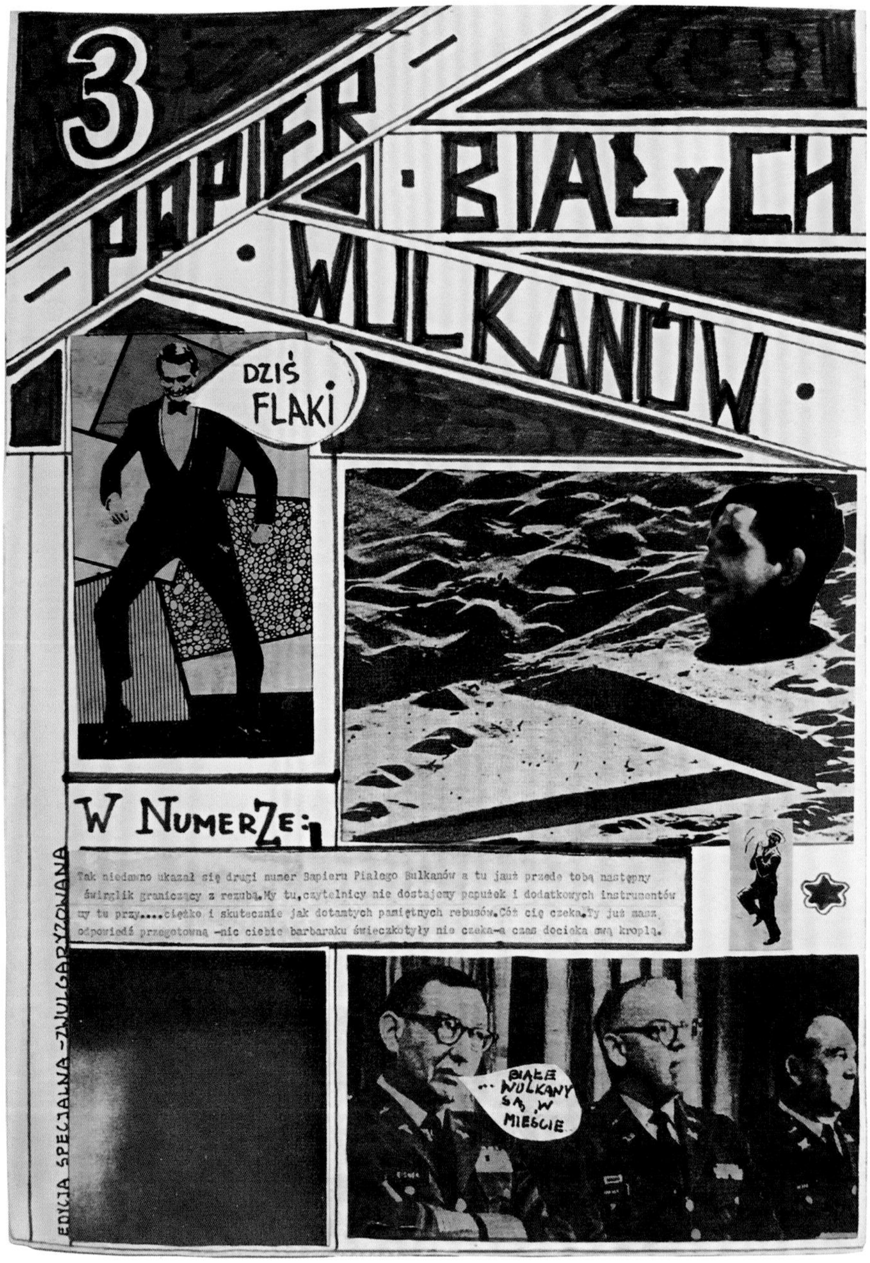

***Papier Białych Wulkanów* (*White Volcano Paper*)**, Warsaw, 1980–1981, published by Jacek 'Luter' Lenartowicz, the drummer of Tilt and Białe Wulkany (White Volcanos).

17. Christian Schmidt, "Meanings of fanzines in the beginning of Punk in the GDR and FRG" in *Volume!* [online], 5:1 (2006). Accessed 15 February 2019.

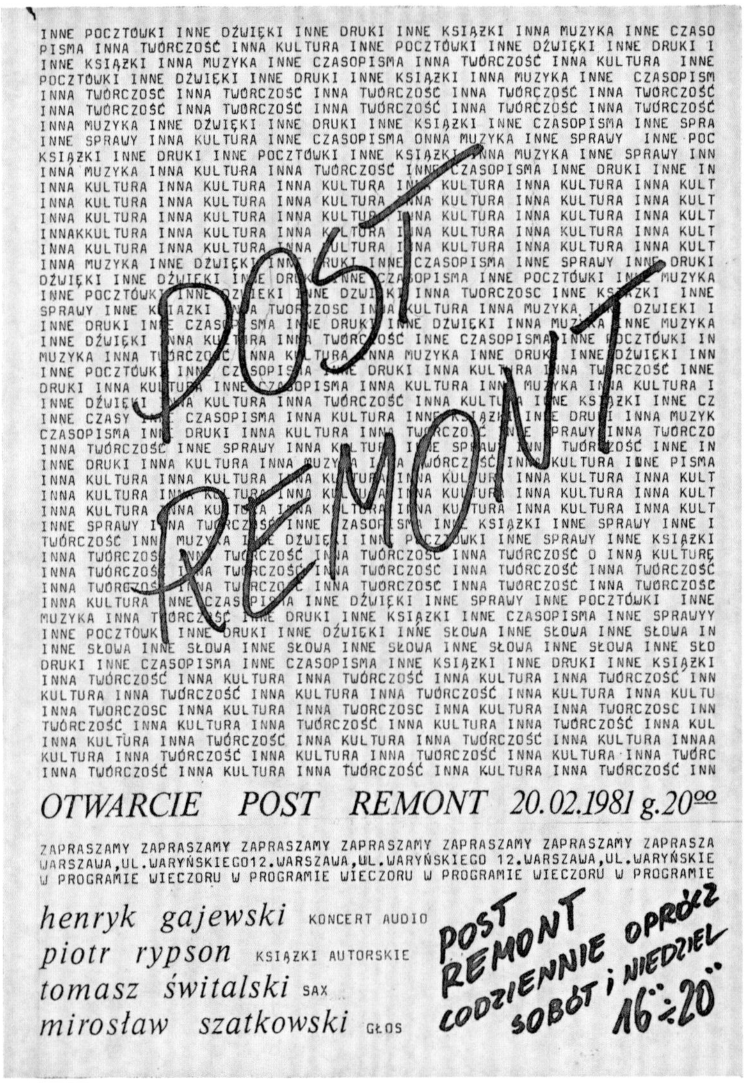

Post Remont, Warsaw, 20 February 1981.
Published by Henryk Gajewski.

Post, No. 6, Warsaw, 10 January 1981.
Published by Henryk Gajewski.

Szmata project, illustration by Piotr Kalon Sawicki.

In the People's Republic of Poland, the chief promotor of punk was Henryk Gajewski, an artist, filmmaker, and curator who had once announced a visit of Andy Warhol to his Warsaw gallery – a notorious prank.[18] Disdainful of the influence of "dilettantes from the radio and discotheques" and the anaemic fare offered by the state record labels, he called for DIY creativity: "Write a text, form a melody, start a band, organise a concert, buy 100 cassettes and reproduce your recording."[19] His appeal was heard, it seems. Some tens of punk fanzines were created between 1979 and the end of the regime, sometimes recycling images and reports from the Western music press, or slicing in material from the Polish press, usually accompanied by a sardonic comment or an absurd image. Often surviving for only one or two issues, fanzines like *PUNK*, *Post*, and *Post Remont* published by Gajewski, *Kanał Review* by Andrzej 'Amok' Turczynowicz, *Zjadacz Radia* and *Papier Białych Wulkanów* by Jacek 'Luter' Lenartowicz, *Organ* by Tomasz Hornung, Stefan 'Mikes' Mikulski's *Szmata*, as well as *Radio Złote Kłosy* by 'Ada' Dąbrowska were typically printed illicitly on duplicating machines, and latterly on photocopiers that were often in workplaces.

18. Łukasz Ronduda, *Sztuka Polska lat 70. Awangarda* (Warsaw and Jelenia Góra: Centrum Sztuki Współczesnej Zamek Ujazdowski, Polski Western, 2009), p. 367.

19. Gajewski cited by Raymond A. Patton in *Punk Crisis: The Global Punk Rock Revolution* (Oxford: Oxford University Press, 2018), p. 47.

Mały Konspirator, Wrocław, 1983. A practical guide on how to react when arrested. Cover illustration by Zbigniew Wołek.

Gajewski's call to action reflected not only his involvement in the networked democracy of Mail Art and his enthusiasm for punk, it also chimed with the rise of independent media in Poland, which had grown in step with the rise of the anti-communist opposition.[20] By the end of the 1970s, an extensive network of independent publications – known as *Drugi Obieg* (*Second Circulation*) – was in place in the People's Republic, contesting the state's grip on information. Works of fiction, historical studies, political philosophy and religious studies, as well as newspapers, were printed and distributed in large numbers, entirely bypassing censorship. Often printed on thin, pulpy paper, what these publications lacked in terms of design and print quality they made up for by affording thrilling access to prohibited knowledge and ideas. When the independent Solidarity Trade Union formed at the very end of the 1970s, the reach of independent media expanded further: unofficial "radio" broadcasts, for instance, were played through the loudspeakers of state factories. Even after Martial Law was declared in December 1981 to suppress Solidarity (*Solidarność*) and restore communist authority, production quickly revived – with estimates of 200 underground newspapers being published in 1983, as well as practical guides on how to react when arrested (*Mały Konspirator*), and even a couple of years later, a comic book version of George Orwell's *Animal Farm*.[21]

So well developed was independent publishing in the People's Republic of Poland that samizdat publishers came from neighbouring countries to learn how

Folwark zwierzęcy, Komiks wg Orwella (**Animal Farm. Comics After Orwell**), samizdat comic book, 1985.

20. See H. Gordon Skilling, *Samizdat and an Independent Society in Central and Eastern Europe* (Columbus: Ohio State University Press, 1989) and Friederike Kind-Kovács and Jessie Labov, eds., *Samizdat, Tamizdat, and Beyond: Transnational Media During and After Socialism* (New York: Berghahn Books, 2013).

21. Czesław Bielecki, Jan Krzysztof Kelus and Urszula Sikorska, *Mały konspirator. poradnik dla dorosłych i młodzieży* (Lublin: Wolne Dźwięki, 1983); *Folwark zwierzęcy* (*Według Orwella*) edited and illustrated by Maciek Biały and Karol Blue (Warsaw: ReKontra, 1985).

to print in volume using offset machines and screen printing facilities. Gábor Demszky and Lászlό Rajk of the AB Kiadó (AB Press) independent publishing house came from Hungary in 1980 to learn how to print in large volume to improve on the "traditional" samizdat method of copying texts on a typewriter charged with sandwiches of thin paper sheets and carbon copy paper. They came back home equipped for screen printing, stencilling, the offset technique, and a Polish speciality – the so-called *ramka* – which involves stretching stencil paper on a frame and impressing it by hand. Rajk also ran a "samizdat boutique" from his flat on Galamb utca in Budapest. Open every week, visitors could view independently published titles and order copies for collection on their return.

GRAPHIC NOISE

Vokno, No. 15, 1989. A Czechoslovak samizdat magazine published by František Stárek.

Punk, it seems, *ought* to have had an affinity with the dissenting cultures that had been in operation in most Eastern Bloc countries for a decade or more, even if none reached the scale of production of Poland around 1980. But along with the new wave subculture that followed in its wake, punk displayed little enthusiasm for authority. And a Xeroxed fanzine or a bootleg tape would simply seem to be a version of samizdat (unlicensed self-publishing) and *magnitizdat* (recordings on tape, typically of live performances by poets and folk musicians). Often, however, the anti-communist opposition cast a wary eye on punks, distrustful of what they saw as their nihilistic and hedonistic attitudes. Others saw in punk a tendency towards compromise and compliance. It lacked the commitment of *opposition*. Writing under the pseudonym Drahomír Křehký in *Vokno*, a Czechoslovak samizdat magazine, Paul Wilson contrasted the new phenomenon of punk and the underground culture which had formed in the early 1970s (in which he had played a part as a member of the underground rock band Plastic People of the Universe). His long article was accompanied by a rogues' gallery of portraits featuring Johnny Rotten and Sid Vicious of the Sex Pistols, as well as other London punks. Written in November 1977, the year he was exiled from Czechoslovakia, Wilson was already well informed about the ways that punk had become pop in the West:

> *The rejection of the values of the establishment is a common attitude of both movements, but while a nicely wrapped rejection can become a commodity in England, it becomes a crime in Czechoslovakia. The Prague musical underground preceded punk by several years, [not because of] any innate characteristics of Czech thought, but rather thanks to the draconian "normalisation" policy of Husák's regime – the policy that forced everyone with really normal artistic expression to hide their existence in the existence of the cracks and crevices of society. The result is that the aesthetic attitude of the underground is, in comparison, much more stubborn and interesting than the punk attitude, which, no matter how intransigent, seems to always leave open a possibility to be devoured by a stronger wave. This is quite normal in the West,*

KRIWET, *Text Dia*, 1970. Installation view at the 33rd Ljubljana Biennial of Graphic Arts, 2019.

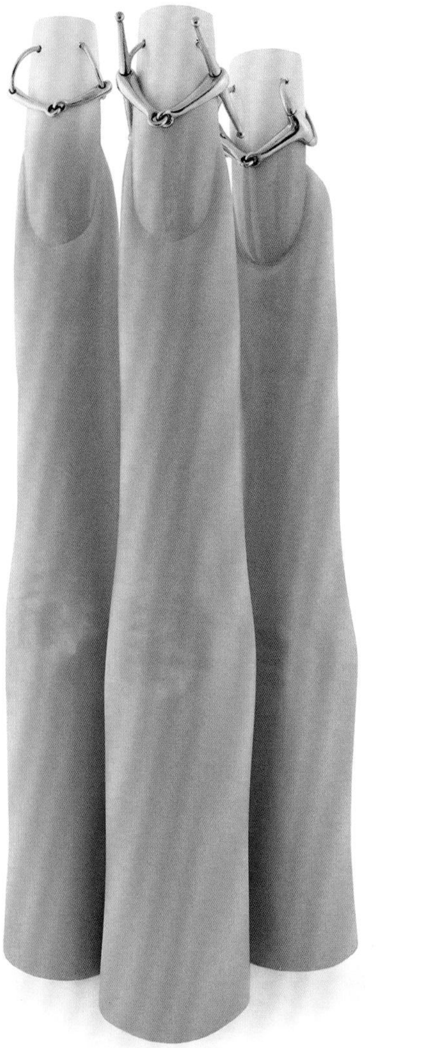

Anna Uddenberg, ***Finger V***, 2018.

Honore Daumier, ***Gargantua***, lithography, 1831. After François Rabelais' humorous novel *Gargantua and Pantagruel*, which explored the excesses and toxicities of its day.

> *from today's rebel becomes tomorrow's manager, and, in the end, it does not have to be bad because it at least ensures that the official culture [in the West] is again revived through self-serving injections of energy and inventiveness. In today's Czechoslovakia, this cannot happen, which is the main reason why the official culture is dead.*[22]

In his review of Czechoslovak underground publishing, Martin Machovec was reluctant to grant "graphomaniac prattling, babbling rubbish" the status of samizdat. Underground printing – or perhaps, the risk of prosecution – carried a kind of gravitas.[23] It was serious business. The publication of works of literature that had been prohibited (such as the novels of Orwell, Bulgakov, and Kafka, for instance) and studies of historical episodes that the authorities would have rather left unexamined (such as the Katyn Massacre, the repression of the Hungarian Uprising in 1956) was a way of righting wrongs. And publishing political philosophy and religious tracts (the Jehovah's Witnesses were particularly busy underground printers) was a means by which the horizons of intellectual life could be elevated. But seriousness was not the defining characteristic of samizdat. In fact, the term itself was coined in the Soviet Union as a parody of the acronyms given to state publishing houses (like Gosizdat and Gostransidat). It also sounded not unlike a brand of popular Georgian wine (Sam-trest). Some samizdat scholars have been keen to emphasise its engagement with the carnivalesque, noting that Mikhail Bakhtin's book on Francois Rabelais and the carnivalesque was published in this underground format in mid 1960s.[24] And samizdat publishers in the Soviet Union took pleasure seriously too,

22. Drahomír Křehký, "Punk Rock" in *Vokno* 1 (1977), p. 43.

23. Martin Machovec, "The Types and Functions of Samizdat Publications in Czechoslovakia, 1948–1989" in *Poetics Today* 30:1 (Spring 2009), p. 6.

24. See Ann Komaromi, "The Material Existence of Soviet Samizdat" in *Slavic Review*, 63:3 (Autumn 2004), pp. 597–618.

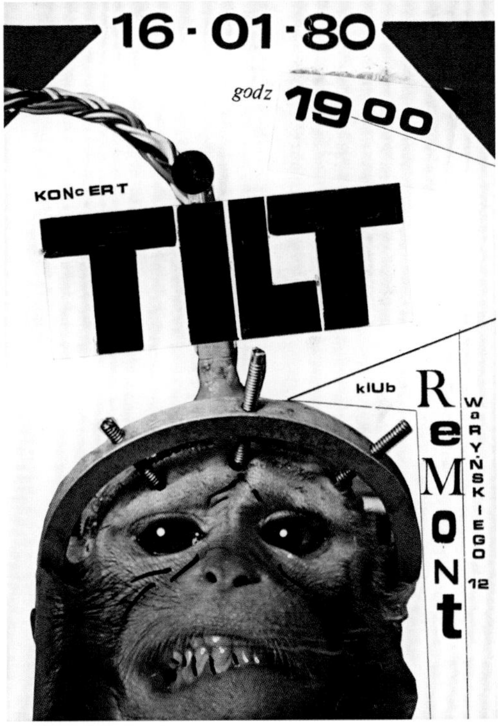

Poster for a Tilt concert at Remont, 1980.

publishing the Kama Sutra and other practical sex guides, histories of jazz music and *Roksi*, a long-running magazine which reported on rock music in the U.S.S.R. and in the West. (First published in just five coverless copies in 1977, each issue probably did not exceed twenty copies in its fifteen-year history.[25])

Punk zines displayed precisely the graphomaniac qualities which Machovec rejected. Combining collaged, scrawled handwriting and a self-consciously amateur appearance, these black and white publications were generally as difficult to read as their counterparts in the West. Rational discourse was eschewed in favour of absurd humour and raucous design. The first issue of *Papier Białych Wulkanów* (*White Volcano Paper*), issued in Warsaw by Jacek 'Luter' Lenartowicz, the drummer of Tilt and Białe Wulkany (White Volcanos), was introduced in 1980–1981, with a question: "What exactly is a white volcano?" The answer was given by Professor Lisol McWhite, a fictional expert in the fictional science of White Volcano Therapy: "White is white, and the volcano is simply a volcano?" Other pages included asemic writing and "cut-up" sentences in the manner of William S. Burroughs. Such devices functioned, according to Dick Hebdige, an early theorist of punk, as "noise": promising communication, they refused to deliver a "message".[26]

This refusal to make direct political statements was particularly striking during periods when the tension between state and society was high. Luxus, a group with a darkly sardonic name, formed during a student strike at the Art Academy in Wrocław, Poland, in 1982.[27] That year Poland was under martial law, introduced by the authorities to put an end to the Solidarity Trade Union: a curfew operated, riot police suppressed protests and strikes, food disappeared from the shops, and letters and phone calls were monitored. The Wrocław group operated as a loose alliance that produced exhibitions by seemingly organising trash; an occasional magazine created with the most primitive means; performances featuring unskilled musicians; and non-camera movies. Luxus was, in effect, a kind of strategy to provide what could not be found anywhere. Speaking in the 1990s Paweł Jarodzki, one of the founders of the group, recalled:

> *… It was martial law, it might have continued for the next fifty years or so for all we knew and perhaps I'd never get to go to America, never get a chance to be as successful as Mr. Warhol … or perhaps I don't feel like it … I don't know. Anyway, I live here and now, and it is here and now that I need to provide myself with … luxury. Everyone wants to be young, rich, have nice girlfriends and lead a nice life in general, and that is something that you need to achieve yourself. So we started an American magazine. American as a concept. The radio played shit, so we recorded Kaman and released those tapes, and played them back at home.*[28]

All of this set them apart from the authors of highly sombre and symbolic art produced in response to the military clamp-down, and crosses, saints, and other martyrological symbols prevailed. They rejected the tidy distinction between state and opposition, one recalling, "We were independent and careless because we did not care" – a sentiment which could have been borrowed from The Ramones.[29]

25. Polly McMichael, "'After all, you're a rock and roll star (at least, that's what they say)': Roksi and the Creation of the Soviet Rock Musician" in *Slavonic and East European Review* 83:4 (2005), pp. 664–684.

26. Dick Hebdige, *Subculture: The Meaning of Style* (London and New York: Routledge, 2002), pp. 99–100.

27. The group had a shifting line-up over its history (1982 to 1995) but the most active members were Paweł Jarodzki (who gave its name), Ewa Ciepielewska and Bożena Grzyb-Jarodzka, as well as Jerzy Kosałka, Marek Czechowski, Artur Gołacki, Małgorzata Plata, Stanisław Sielicki, Jacek Jankowski, Szymon Lubiński, Andrzej Jarodzki, and Krzysztof Kłosowicz (aka Kaman).

28. "Rzeczywistość się penetruje", Wojciech Bockenheim's interview with Paweł Jarodzki in *bruLion* 16 (1991), pp. 74–75, cited in Anna Mituś and Piotr Stasiowski, eds., *Agresywna niewinność: Historia grupy LUXUS* (Wrocław: BWA Galerie Sztuki Współczesnej, 2014), p. 33.

29. Ewa Ciepielewska cited by Anna Markowska, "Laughter at War" in Ann Murray, ed., *Constructing the Memory of War in Visual Culture since 1914: The Eye on War* (London and New York: Routledge, 2018), pp. 81–82.

Luxus formed brief alliances with musicians in the city, including Miki Mausoleum and Zad Gumowego Wieloryba. Their handmade zine – printed on pages intended for army newspapers or stolen blocks of perforated computer paper, and featuring stencils, linocuts, and rubdown and hand lettering – was also a group effort. Brimming with colour and exuberant sloganeering in support of the army, pornography, or American cinema, the artzine *Luxus* approached the curfews, censorship, and shortages under martial law and the tasks of opposition with irreverence.

Luxus. The International Political 'n Fucking magazine, No. 4, undated.

When it first appeared, punk was usually characterised by its critics as a sign of degeneration and corruption. The state security services in Czechoslovakia, for instance, launched a campaign against punks with the code name *Odpad* (Waste).[30] Parodying early press reports in Slovenia, Žižek wrote: "Lyrics ooze with nihilistic, self-destructive protest, charged with cheap provocations: instead the youth should focus their critical energy in a more constructive direction." This image of suppuration was well observed. Punks frequently embraced abjection, with bands adopting names like Gnile Duše (Rotten Souls) in Yugoslavia, and a Czech fanzine called *Sracka* (*Shit*). One of the earliest punk songs in the Soviet Union invited society to "shit on my face".[31] Declarations of self-abasement, images of waste and decay were common in punk in the West too, but they carried all the more force in the East in societies which claimed to be based on a "scientific", progressive ideology. If punk was, as Žižek declared, a social symptom, then its interest in waste and entropy might best be understood as another expression of the stagnation (*zastoia* in Russian) which is so often used to tag the Brezhnev period.

30. Miroslav Vaněk, *Ostrůvky svobody: kulturní a občanské aktivity mladé generace v 80. letech v Československu* (Praha: Ústav pro soudobé dějiny AV ČR, 2002), p. 193.

31. Egor Letov "Nasrat' na moe litso" ("Shit on my face") from the album *Totalitarizm'* (*Totalitarianism*), 1987.

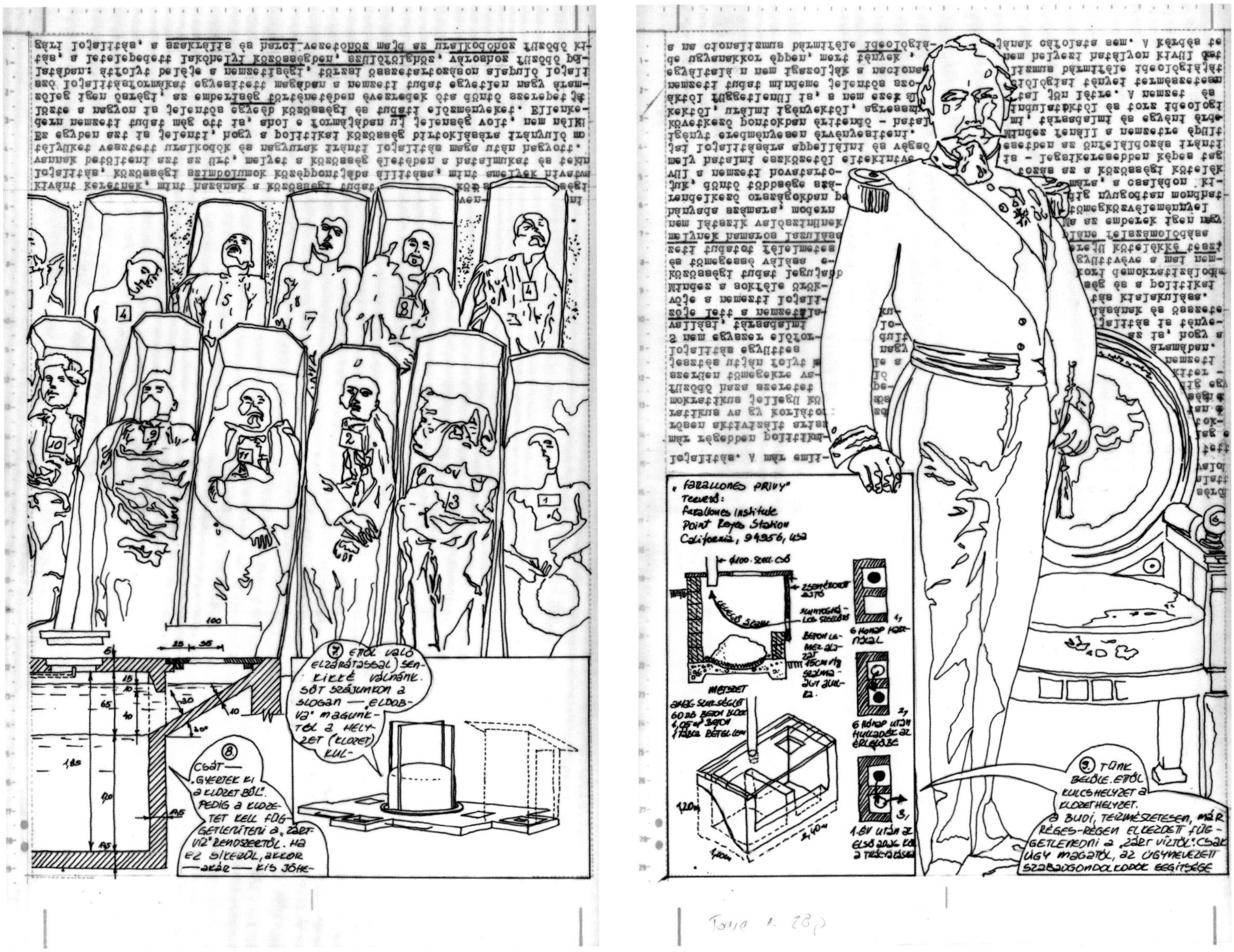

Laszlo Rajk, ***Kulczhelyzet*** (***Key Position***), unpublished samizdat, 1983. The line drawings depict Andre Adolphe Eugene Disderi's photograph of dead communards and Jean Hippolyte Flandrin's portrait of Napolean III.

László Rajk, founder of the Samizdat Boutique in Budapest, brought these themes together when he proposed that AB Kiadó, the independent publisher of Václav Havel and Milan Kundera's works in Hungary, as well as serious studies into minority rights, published his comic book *Kulczhelyzet* (*Key Position*, 1983).[32] The history of the improvement of the WC is told in a series of line drawings which combine technical designs with the contours of famous images depicting the battles and class struggles of the 19th-century. They include dead communards in their coffins in Andre Adolphe Eugene Disderi's famous photograph (1871); Jean-Francois Millet's weary *Man with a Hoe* (1862) and Jean Hippolyte Flandrin's portrait of Napoleon III (1861). Istvan Bibó's semi-psychoanalytical study of the failure of democracy and what he called "*elmaradottság*" (backwardness) in the region, *A kelet-európai kisállamok nyomorúsága* (*The Misery of Small Eastern European States*, 1946) forms a typed

32. Gábor Demszky, László Rajk, and Edit Sasvári, *Földalatti vonalak* (Budapest: Jelenkor Kiadó, 2000).

backdrop to Rajk's images. Evading a clear message, Rajk seems to ask: What is progress? Revolutionary politics or flushing toilets? Lacking the noisiness of punk, it nevertheless entertained some of its ironic coprophilia. In the end, *Kulczhelyzet* was not published, failing to find approval with the AB Kiadó editorial board.

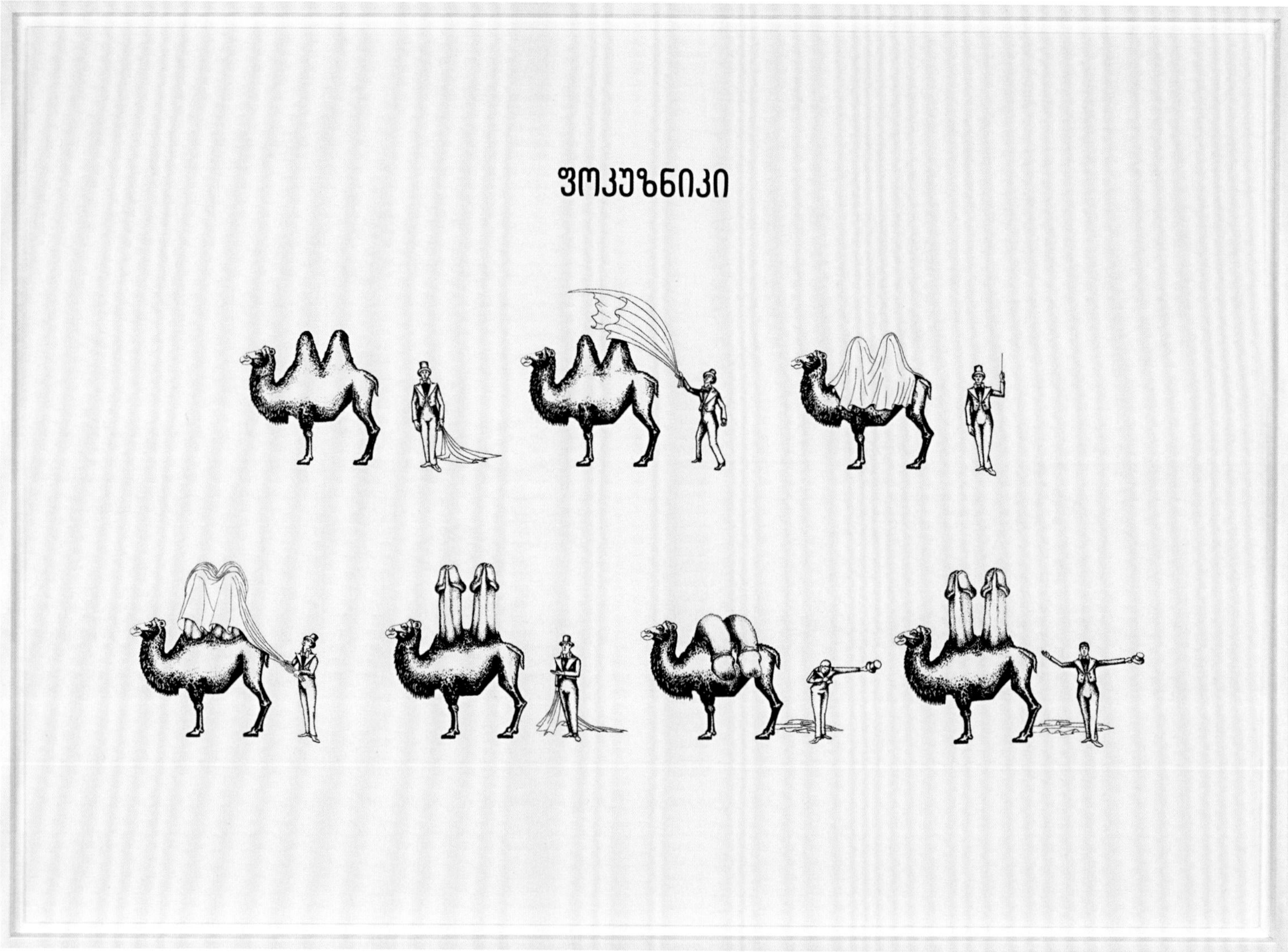

Giorgi Xaniashvili, ***Untitled***, 2019. From the Print Portfolio, The 33rd Ljubljana Biennial of Graphic Arts, 2019.

QUEERING SOCIALISM

Punk and new wave often channelled sexual "deviance" too, sometimes in the deployment of the illicit iconography of sexual fetishism or by perverting gender conventions. The third punk issue of *Problemi* in Slovenia (1983) featured illustrations of erotic asphyxiation (a translation of an article from the Italian magazine, *Fridigaire*); the sadomaschostic lyrics of tracks by Borghesia, an early electronic music group; and a set of photographs by Miki Stojković of a man and topless woman playing with a large five-pointed star, the primary symbol of Titoism, under the title "Revolution is a Whore". Many of the authors of this material in *Problemi* were associated with FV 112/15, a theatre group established in 1980 by Neven Korda and Zemira Alajbegović. Abandoning the stage, FV 112/15 evolved rapidly into something like a multimedia platform for the production of alternative forms of culture, much in the DIY-spirit of punk. It released records and cassettes through its music label, and in 1982 it established a regular club night in Ljubljana, Disko FV; four members (Dario Seraval, Aldo Ivančić, Korda, and Alajbegović) formed Borghesia, a band which achieved international success on the electronic music scene in the late 1980s. FV 112/15 also organised Magnus, a festival of gay and lesbian films in 1984. According to Korda, the group was not interested in shifting mainstream cultural practices and values, instead it staked out a zone where the conventions of Yugoslav life did not seem to apply, though happily drawing resources from state-funded institutions when needed (for instance, borrowing the cameras owned by the local student centre).[33]

Viks, No. 2, entitled "Homosexuality and Culture", issued on the opening day of the Magnus Film Festival, 1984.

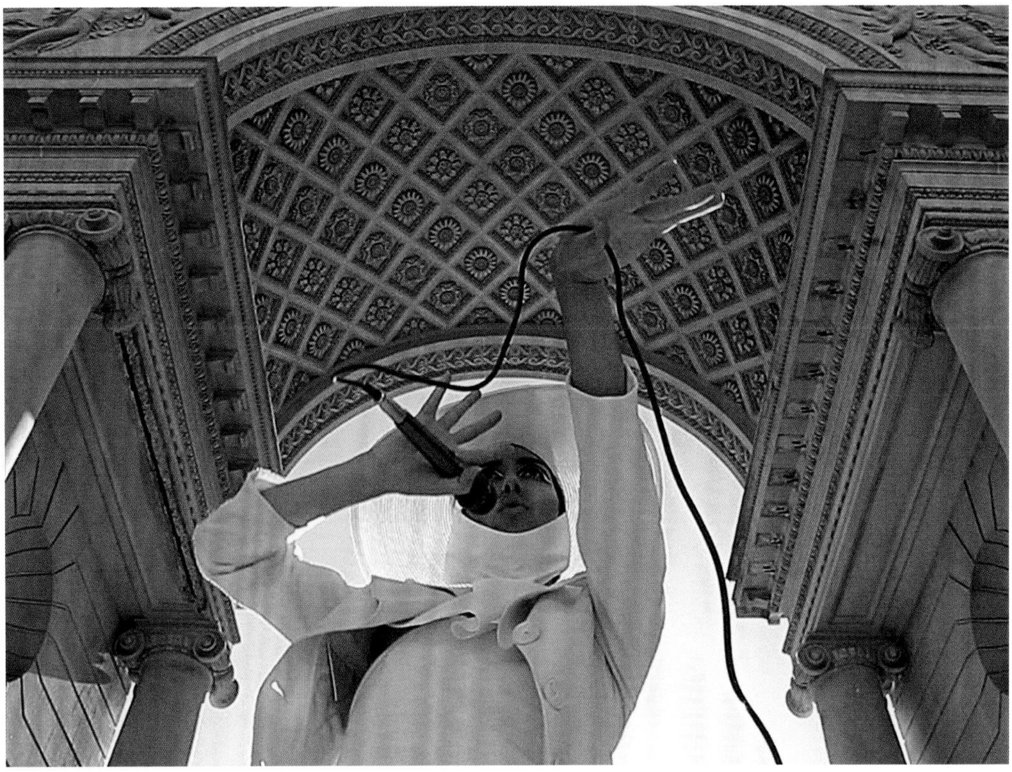

Martine Gutierrez, ***Martine Part I-IX***, 2012–2016 (still).

One of the defining features of the alternative culture that formed in Ljubljana in the early 1980s were the short films and videos – akin to pop videos on the then new MTV channel – made by FV members like Korda and Alajbegović. Barbara Borčić notes that much of the material that the FV artists snatched for their video projects featured "recognisable political personalities, rituals and manifestations including Tito's funeral, or popular Yugoslav music stars", as well as "shots from pornographic movies recorded from private Italian

33. Neven Korda, "FV and the 'Third Scene' 1980–1990" in Liljana Stepančič and Breda Škrjanec, eds., *FV Alternativa osemdesetih* (Ljubljana: Mednarodni grafični likovni center, 2008), p. 312.

Dozie Kanu, ***Chair [iii] (Crack Rock Beige)***, 2018 (front). XIYADIE, ***Sorting sweet potatoes (Dad, don't yell, we're in the cellar sorting sweet potatoes)***, 2019 (back). Installation view at the 33rd Ljubljana Biennial of Graphic Arts, 2019.

Vladislav Mamyshev-Monroe, ***Life of great Monroes***, 1996.

Vladislav Mamyshev-Monroe, ***Gorbachev***, from the *Politburo series*, 1990.

television programmes."[34] Early video works like Korda's *Obnova* (*Renewal, 6*, 1983) – compiled from clips emphasising the industrial rhythms of sex in pornography – and Zemira Alajbegović's *Tereza* (*4*, 1983) – in which TV footage of socialist ceremonies is intercut with popular melodramas – could be filed under the voguish category of "appropriation art". But another way of understanding this material is to see it as a queering of Yugoslav socialism. FV videos and performances sought to unsettle the normative effects of state media, sometimes by eroticising its heroes and sacred symbols. Recalling her activities in the orbit of FV at the time (particularly the video works made with Šmid), Gržinić writes: "queer positions – every form of non-heterosexual positioning – we understood, exclusively and entirely, as a political stance. This queerness – and the word queer means literally 'not right / not quite' – demands, of us and of the viewer, a rethinking of the conditions of life, work, and possibilities of resistance."[35]

The last expression of what might be called "punky samizdat" in the Soviet Union also embraced queerness. Piratskoe Televidenie (Pirate TV) was a video platform formed by young artists and musicians in Leningrad at the end of the 1980s. With new-found access to VCRs and video cameras, the artists Yuris Lesnik, Timur Novikov, and Vladimir Mamyshev-Monroe made improvised and uncensored "programmes" that had the liveliness and busy energy of MTV, if not its production values. Their programmes were self-published, copied on domestic VCR machines and shared in their networks. Assuming a feminine appearance (in make-up and wearing a dress fashioned from glossy black LPs), Mamyshev-Monroe hosted two series, *Culture News* and *The Deaths of Famous People* (an inversion of a well-known series of books in the U.S.S.R., *Lives of Famous People*). In one, Mamyshev (Marilyn) appears, flirting naked with the video camera in the bath and singing to a figure in a JFK mask: "Miss Monroe, I am paralysed by your beauty", he says. "Me too", replies the dead film star.

Mamyshev-Monroe's first appearances had been as an on-stage model with the Pop Mechanics orchestra, a seemingly chaotic ensemble that was formed by piano virtuoso Sergey Kuryokhin in Leningrad in 1984. Mamyshev-Monroe would appear as a vision of Marilyn in the midst of raucous performances featuring groups of punk and new wave musicians and jazz players, as well as military bands and even live animals. Rejecting the fascination with crossdressing pop stars who were starting to appear in Soviet culture (the "quagmire of transvestism"), Mamyshev-Monroe started a career as an artist by queering the icons of history, politics, and popular culture. Mamyshev-Monroe assumed a hybrid persona combining Adolf Hitler and Marilyn-Monroe, dissolving "both of them in myself, this appearing as the model of the new man." "Through all my physical and mental mechanism to embody mankind in all its variety," he claimed to "experience all these destinies myself, take on myself all these countless sins, neutralise these with countless good deeds, eliminate sexual, national, social differences and remain myself in this singular variety."[36]

Not just content with raising icons from the past, Mamyshev-Monroe also embraced the hero of the day, Mikhail Gorbachev. As General Secretary of the Communist Party of the Soviet Union, Gorbachev had launched the

34. Barbara Borčić, "Video Art from Conceptualism to Postmodernism" in Dubravka Djurić, ed., *Impossible Histories: Historical Avant-gardes, Neo-avant-gardes, and Post-avant-gardes in Yugoslavia, 1918–1991* (Boston: MIT press, 2003), p. 514.

35. Marina Gržinić, "The Video, Film, and Interactive Multimedia Art of Marina Gržinić and Aina Šmid, 1982–2008" in Marina Gržinić, Tanja Velagić, eds., *The Video Art of Marina Gržinić and Aina Šmid*, trans. Rawley Grau (Vienna: Erhard Löcker GesmbH, 2008), p. 48.

36. Vladislav Mamyshev (Monroe-Hitler), "Where the Heck am I? Where are my things?" in Viktor Mazin, ed., *Kabinet: An Anthology* (St. Petersburg: Ina-press and Amsterdam: Stedelijk Museum, 1997), p. 110.

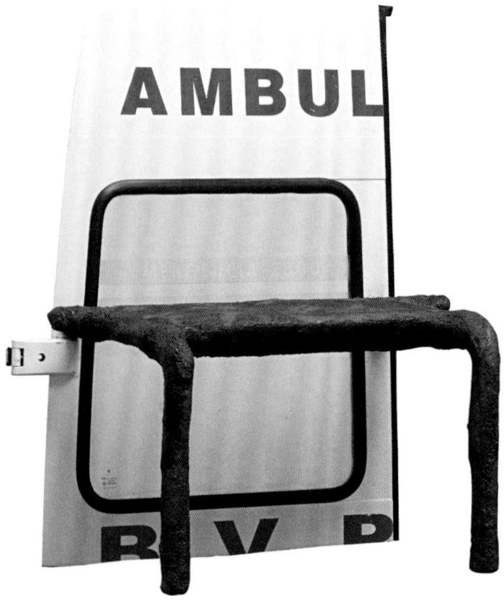

Dozie Kanu, ***Chair* [*xiv*] (*Imobilidade M'aider*)**, 2019.

policies of *glasnost* (openness) and *perestroika* (restructuring) in 1986, introducing an unprecedented degree of permissiveness and cultural autonomy in a country that was better known for censorship and control. Ten standard photographic portraits of members of the current Soviet Politbureau – including that of Gorbachev – were "made-over" by Mamyshev-Monroe with lipstick, jewellery, and elaborate graphic hairstyles, and they hung in Evgeny Kozlov's studio in Leningrad in 1990. There, they attracted the attention of the international press, looking for easily conveyed symbols of artistic freedom in a fast-changing Soviet Union. In this way, a queered image of a feminine Gorbachev appeared around the world. In fact, Mamyshev-Monroe's Politbureau portraits joined a large body of Western reports breathlessly describing the fast changes in the Soviet Union then underway. The eccentric Soviet punk and new wave style often featured in these articles, and provided a spectacular contrast with the drabness of Soviet streets and homes. Moreover, the punk phenomenon, already a decade old, was immediately legible to Western readers. It seems an odd paradox of history that the reassurance of familiarity could be provided by an aesthetic that had been created to stir controversy.

URŠULA THE WITCH

Uršula is a witch rumoured to live in a cave in Slivnica, a hill overlooking the town of Cerknica.

She is said to create storms in the valley below, and is the mother of the Slivnica Mountain witches. Lake Cerknica is an "intermittent lake", as it drains during the autumn through its bed of porous karst limestone. The vanishing lake gave rise to folkloric speculation that the phenomenon was due to supernatural forces. In the 17th-century, the Slovenian historian and polymath Baron Janez Vajkard Valvasor (1641–1693) wrote about the Slivnica Mountain witches in describing the social and natural history of Lake Cerknica and the surrounding region. Uršula is also a central figure at the annual Pust celebrations (the Slovenian carnival that extends from Shrove Sunday to Ash Wednesday) in Cerknica. During these celebrations, the town changes its name to Butale, after the fictional town in Fran Milčinski's collection of satirical stories, *Butalci*, and is said to transfer municipal authority to the conductor of the carnival for this time. Uršula is invited to the festival every year in order for residents to bring an end to winter and usher in the springtime. The parade begins with the so-called "sawing of the witch", where participants cut up a large papier mâché sculpture of Uršula. Residents costumed as witches, Butalci, and other masked satirical figures then parade the streets.

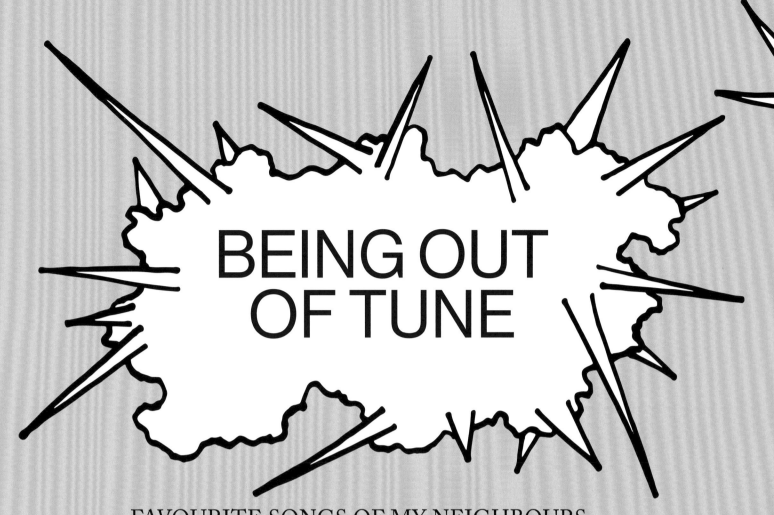

BEING OUT OF TUNE

FAVOURITE SONGS OF MY NEIGHBOURS, ABUSERS, AND DESPOTS

AUGUSTIN MAURS

Being Out of Tune is a parodic recital based on songs that have been used, abused, and co-opted by ruling powers or performed by political leaders. Playing with the notions of consonance and dissonance, the piece deals with musical interconnections among popular, populist, and totalitarian forces. The songs are understood as found objects, set in a cabaret show where the act of singing has been problematised.

Augustin Maurs, ***Being out of Tune: Favourite songs of my neighbours, abusers and despots***, concert part of the public programme of the 33rd Ljubljana Biennial of Graphic Arts, 2019.

ÖŇE, ÖŇE DIŇE ÖŇE JAN WATANYM TÜRKMENISTANYM

Hormatly Prezidentimiz Gurbanguly Berdimuhamedow
Öňe, öňe diňe öňe jan Watanym
Türkmenistanym!

Parahatlyk-ýürek baydagy
Älem-jahan mähir mukamy
Türkmenistan bahar baýramy
Türkmenistan dostluk mekany.

Öňe, öňe diňe öňe jan Watanym
Türkmenistanym

Ajap eýýam, ajap çagym bar,
Ýalkym saçýan şamçyragym bar
Hak sylamyş Beyik Gerçegiň
Gahryman halkymyz bar.

SETLIST

Meglio 'na Canzone
(Silvio Berlusconi and Mariano Apicella, Italy)
Frequently performed by Silvio Berlusconi.

Öňe, öňe diňe öňe jan Watanym Türkmenistanym
(Gurbanguly Berdimuhamedow, Turkmenistan)
Composed and performed by the president of Turkmenistan, Gurbanguly Berdimuhamedow. A choir of 4,166 people broke a world record by singing this song in a choreographed show in Turkmenistan, 2015.

Ikaw
(Pilita Corrales, Philippines)
Performed by Rodrigo Duterte in a duet with Pilita Corrales at Donald Trump's request during the ASEAN Summit in Manila, 2017.

IKAW

Ikaw ang bigay ng maykapal
Tugon sa aking dasal
Upang sa lahat ng panahon
Bawat pagkakataon
Ang ibigin ko'y ikaw
Ikaw ang tanglaw sa 'king mundo
Kabiyak nitong puso ko
Wala ni kahati mang saglit
Na sa yo'y maipapalit
Ngayo't kailanma'y ikaw
Ang lahat ng aking galaw
Ang sanhi ay ikaw
Kung may bukas mang tinatanaw
Dahil may isang ikaw
Kulang ang magpakailan pa man
Upang bawat sandali ay
Upang muli't muli ay
Ang mahalin ay ikaw

Awara Hoon
(Raj Kapoor, India)
Reportedly Mao Zedong's favourite song.

Blutrote Rosen
(Austin Egen, Germany)
A favourite song of Adolf Hitler.

My Way
(Frank Sinatra, U.S.)
The song that Slobodan Milošević repeatedly listened to while detained for war crimes in The Hague.

Blueberry Hill
(Fats Domino, U.S.)
Performed by Vladimir Putin during a charity event in Saint Petersburg, 2010.

***Сулико* (*Suliko*)**
(old Georgian folk song)
Joseph Stalin's favourite song.

***СУЛИКО* (*SULIKO*)**

Я искал могилу милой,
обошёл я все края.
И рыдал слезой горючей:
“Где ты, милая моя?”

Я в кустах увидел розу
что светилась, как заря.
И спросил её с волненьем:
“Ты ли милая моя?”

Нежно засвистала пташка,
И спросил я соловья:
“Молвы, звонкая пичужка:
Ты желанная моя?”

Соловей склонив головку,
На кустах своих свистал,
Словно ласково ответил:
“Угадал ты – это я”

Les 80 Chasseurs
(old French song)
Sung by Jean-Marie Le Pen at a political gathering in France, 2012.

***Mei Hua* (*Plum Flower*)**
(Teresa Teng, Taiwan)
A beloved song of Chiang Kai-shek.

Brother Louie
(Pochonbo Electronic Ensemble, Democratic People’s Republic of Korea)
Reportedly Kim Jong-un’s favourite song.

Is That All There Is?
(Peggy Lee, U.S.)
A favourite song of President Donald J. Trump.

ABSURDMYSTIC

METAHAVEN

The linguist and philologist Victor Klemperer once noted that words can be "like tiny doses of arsenic" that are "swallowed unnoticed". Klemperer, who was Jewish, hinted at his own, entirely unwitting, adoption of Nazi jargon in his everyday language, apparent from terms such as "extermination" and "work deployment", and collectives such as "the Russian" or "the Jew". Satire should strive to question the very world that is made out of such names and terms.

Our encounter with anonymous Russian children's verses going under the loose genre name of перевертыши (*perevertyshi*, turnarounds) – initially through a collection of Russian children's poetry – happened in rollercoaster days and nights between the sickness and death of a parent, and the early youth and blossoming of a child. These self-negating rhymes, full of contradictions, seemed to us the one thing to make perfect sense of our world:

In January, on the 5th of April,
In dry weather - with knee-high puddles.
On a brick street - made of
wooden planks
Walked a tall man - of short height
Curly with no hair - thin like a barrel.
With no children - only a son and
a daughter.
Writes a letter home:
I'm healthy - in a hospital,
Fed up - and hungry,
All come visit me - I don't want
to see you.[1]

Our friend, the artist and theorist Alex Anikina, wrote:

It is definitely a genre in itself.
You would make them up on the
go usually. One that was popular
in my childhood was:

По реке плывет кирпич,
Деревянный как стекло,
Ну и пусть себе плывет,
Нам не нужен пенопласт.

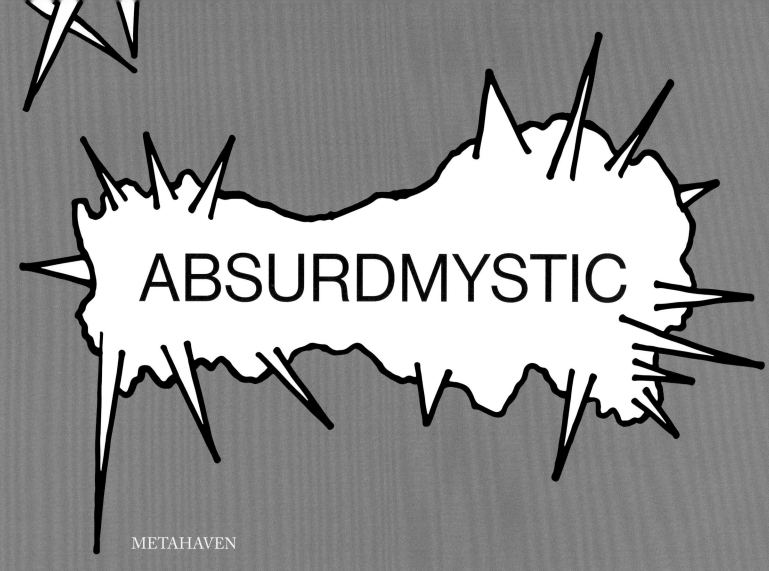

*
This text is a reworked fragment and summary from Metahaven's lecture "Sleep Walks the Street: from memes to Vvedensky" at the *Crack Up – Crack Down* Symposium in Ljubljana. It is part of Metahaven's forthcoming book on art, cinema, analogy, and abstraction. With thanks to Lesia Prokopenko, Eugene Ostashevsky, and Alex Anikina.

1.
Дело было в январе,
пятого апреля,
Сухо было на дворе –
лужи по колено,
По кирпичной мостовой,
сделанной из досок,
Шел высокий гражданин
низенького роста,
Кучерявый, без волос;
худенький, как бочка.
У него детишек нет,
только сын да дочка.
Пишет он домой письмо:
Жив здоров – лежу в
больнице,
Сыт по горло – есть хочу,
Приходите все родные –
я вас видеть не хочу.
Translated from the Russian by Alex Anikina, January 2017.

Alexander Vvedensky (1904–1941).

She continued:

> *It takes well to translation. It's so expressive because the emphasis falls very strongly on the last syllable, but at the same time there is no rhyme. I would translate it:*
>
> *Down the river floats a brick,*
> *Wooden like a sheet of glass,*
> *Let it do its own thing,*
> *We don't need styrofoam.*[2]

Further down the path of this self-negational "absurdism", sharing common mystic ties, lies the writing of Alexander Vvedensky. Vvedensky was a founding member of OBERIU, the "Union for Real Art", a collective of poets that was active in Leningrad in the 1920s and 1930s, meeting its sorrowful end in the early 1940s. The designation "absurdism" is somewhat of a Western misnomer, at least when it comes to OBERIU, writes Eugene Ostashevsky – a poet, scholar, and the main translator of Vvedensky's poetry into the English language. Indeed, what was at work in OBERIU and Vvedensky was something more than simply disorganising the making of meaning.

Alexander Vvedensky developed a rich poetic language that undermined the operative capacity of rhetorical expression. For example, Vvedensky did not merely use metaphor to invoke open-ended poetic imagery; he "materialised" metaphor, revealing the role that words play in assuming a (false) correspondence between language and the world. In *The Gray Notebook*, a concise body of texts that shed light on his artistic and philosophical methodology, Vvedensky wrote about naming processes:

> *Let us think about simple things. We say: tomorrow, today, evening. Thursday, month, year, during the course of the week. We count the hours in a day. We point to their increase. Earlier, we saw only half the day, now we have noticed the movement within the whole of the day. But when the next day comes, we begin counting the hours anew.*

Then, he continues:

> *... in the case of time, its addition differs from all other addition. You can't compare three months you lived through to three trees that have grown again. The trees are right there, their leaves glimmer dimly. Of months you can't say the same with confidence. The names of minutes, seconds, hours, days, weeks, and months distract us from even our superficial understanding of time. All these names are analogous either to objects, or to concepts and measures of space. As a result, a week gone by lies before us like a killed deer.*[3]

you undress like a statue

Metahaven, ***Eurasia* (*Questions on Happiness*)**, 2018 (still). Citation from Alexander Vvedensky, "Snow Lies", 1930, translated from the Russian by Eugene Ostashevsky.

2. Alex Anikina, email to author, January 2017.

3. Alexander Vvedensky, *An Invitation for Me to Think*, selected and translated by Eugene Ostashevsky (New York: NYRB Poets, 2013), p. 74.

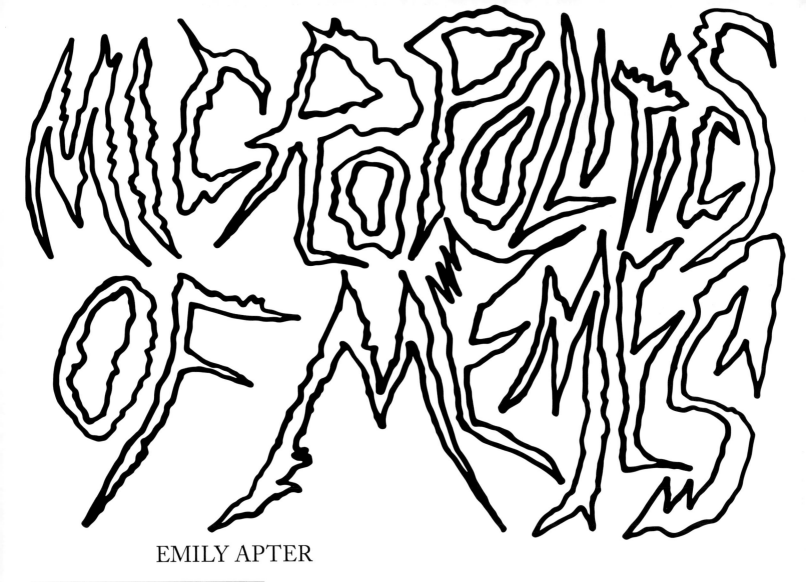

MICROPOLITICS OF MEMES

EMILY APTER

Looney Tunes **opening title as a template for the creation of memes, 2019.**

Can one say anything serious about memes? Are earworms, loony tunes, pet videos, or those random weird things you can't get out of your head anything more than just fodder for empty hours? Or self-medicating forms of humour that take you through the trauma of daily headlines? Memes correspond to what Charles Sanders Peirce called "general predicates of thought". They build strength through repetition and recognition and call attention to themselves through techniques of *likeness, indication, guideposting, exclamation, attention-forcing, thrown-togetherness,* and the status conditions of *badge* or *shibboleth*.[1] Memes also illustrate the thrust of the drives, manifest in the obsessive-compulsive desire to engineer repeat "hits" to consciousness. Peter Szendy describes feeling "haunted, obsessed to the point of queasiness, possessed until you just can't take it any more by one of those tunes that come to you *just like that*, one of those songs you hear by chance … one of those *hits* that, from that moment on, refuses to let you go. … Nothing is to be done: A kind of virus has taken a hold of you … And you have caught what some have called an *earworm* [a translation of the German *Ohrwurm*, used to describe the "musical itch" of the brain]."[2]

Richard Dawkins, who famously coined the neologism "meme" in his 1976 classic *The Selfish Gene*, treated its survival as analogous to natural selection in biological evolution.

1. Charles Sanders Peirce, "What is a Sign?" (1894). https://www.marxists.org/reference/subject/philosophy/works/us/peirce1.htm.

2. Peter Szendy, *Hits: Philosophy in the Jukebox*, trans. Will Bishop (New York: Fordham University Press, 2012), pp. 2–3.

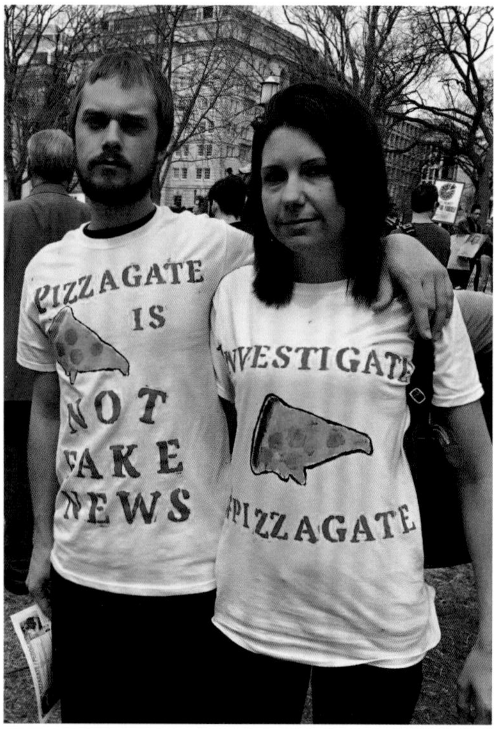

This is what the debunked "Pizzagate" conspiracy theory looks like. The theory went viral during the 2016 U.S. presidential election cycle.

Charles Sanders Peirce, father of semiosis.

> *I think that a new kind of replicator has recently emerged on this very planet. It is staring us in the face. It is still in its infancy, still drifting clumsily about in its primeval soup, but already it is achieving evolutionary change at a rate that leaves the old gene panting far behind. … "Mimeme" comes from a suitable Greek root, but I want a monosyllable that sounds a bit like 'gene.' I hope my classicist friends will forgive me if I abbreviate mimeme to meme. If it is any consolation, it could alternatively be thought of as being related to 'memory,' or to the French word même. It should be pronounced to rhyme with 'cream.'*[3]

Pepe the Frog got busted, 2019.

Though Dawkins would underscore that memes multiply through *non-genetic* reproduction and eventually refute the idea (proposed by N.K. Humphrey) that they are actually existing living structures residing in the brain, he certainly encouraged the conceptual rhyme scheme of meme and gene; it appears throughout the book like a running joke.

Situated midway between Peirce's "predicates of thought" and Dawkins's "selfish gene" there is René Thom's distinction between *saillance* (a disruptive flash or jolt of sensory stimulus) and *pregnance* (animal cues ensuring propagation and species survival). Forged at a particular juncture of French phenomenology and life science in the early 1940s, Thom's speculations on the biological origins of human symbolism yielded the proposition that predication rests on *l'investissement d'une forme saillante par une prégnance*, roughly, "the vesting of a salient form by an expectant substance."[4] The formula is useful for understanding, from the perspective of ethology and "semio-physics", the conditions by which a meme "takes" or becomes a holding-object of the brain. Umberto Eco, for his part, would associate this kind of predictive processing with the workings of the "recognition seme" based on "codes of recognition".

3. Richard Dawkins, *The Selfish Gene* (Oxford: Oxford University Press, 1976, 2006), p. 249.

4. René Thom, *Apologie du logos* (Paris: Hachette, 1940), p. 1.

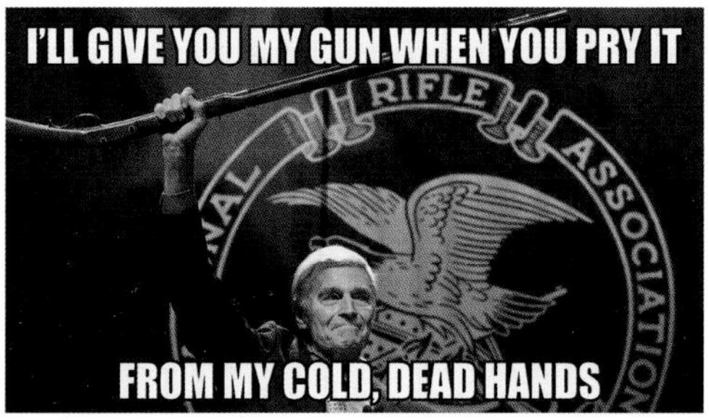

Charlton Heston, five-term president of the National Rifle Association.

> *There is a principle of economy both in the recollection of perceived things and in the recognition of familiar objects, and it is based on what I shall call codes of recognition. These codes list certain features of the object as the most meaningful for purposes of recollection or future communication: for example, I recognize a zebra from a distance without noting the exact shape of the head or the relation between legs and body. It is enough that I recognize two pertinent characteristics – four-leggedness and stripes.*[5]

As objects of gestalt learning and *iconotropy* (the appropriation and reworking of like images), memes are construed by navigating diverse fields and subdisciplines: evolutionary biology, phenomenology, cognitive psychology, semiotics, technologies of neuroimaging, epi- and ontogenetics.[6] With respect to epigenetics, I refer to the way in which the meme, like the interpretive molecule of RNA, reproduces a memory-self through mnemonic traces that pass along inherited trauma. With respect to ontogenetics, I refer to how memes function as operators that hybridise modes of existence, genres and medial forms: jokes, puns, religious icons, transitional objects that soothe and heal. Underscoring this therapeutic capacity, the *Urban Dictionary* notes: "Memes are a lifestyle and art used by teens and adults who are willing to actually live a life that doesn't include depression. Technically the main reason half the world has not committed to die."[7]

In their antidepressant function, memes are salves for solitary souls. They are community-builders, connecting solo agents to social networks and political causes. They engender an implicit trust among the "users" who co-produce and distribute them, and, by doing so, model a kind of sharing economy dubbed "platform cooperativism" by Trebor Scholz.[8] And yet, because of their predication on impersonal intimacy, memes shift the ground of the political, from an ethics of direct responsibility to an ethics of limited liability and indirect consequence in moral action. The emotionally reactive, remotely-responsible meme user profiles the political actor as triumphalist raptor or rogue agent. Not surprisingly, memes enjoy a particularly robust life on the political right, their ever-evolving morphologies in step with the latest strategic political innovations in gerrymandering, voter suppression, "cancellation" on social media, and "computational propaganda" whose objectives include damage to the opponent's reputational brand ("Pizzagate"), and industrial-strength production of triggering tags ("fetal heartbeat", MAGA, the NRA Charlton Heston meme: "I'll give you my gun when you pry it from *my cold, dead hands*").[9] Fully weaponised as technologies of harassment and hate-mongering within a general "cryptoeconomy of affect",[10] memes are omnipresent warriors in the culture / flame wars (to wit, the flashpoint of "Pepe the Frog" after the internet meme's appropriation by the alt-right as ideological mascot for white supremacy and white nationalism).[11]

Of course the right does not own the meme-tool. The "aggressive" character of the meme has been mobilised across the political spectrum (including left on left attacks), channelling the epidemiological analogy to an "aggressive virus" and all that comes with it: imaginaries of disease,

5. Umberto Eco, "Critique of the Image" in Victor Burgin ed., *Thinking Photography* (London and Basingstoke: Macmillan, 1982), p. 33. Originally published in *Cinemantics* 1 (1970).

6. I borrow the term "iconotropy" from Michael Camille's *The Gothic Idol: Ideology and Image-Making in Medieval Art* (Cambridge: Cambridge University Press, 1989), p. 240.

7. "Memes", *Urban Dictionary*. https://www.urbandictionary.com/define.php?term=Memes Accessed 12 June 2019.

8. Trebor Scholz, *Platform Cooperativism: Challenging the Corporate Sharing Environment* (New York: Rosa Luxemburg Stiftung, 2016). https://www.academia.edu/22572831/An_Introduction_to_Platform_Cooperativism

9. I borrow this term from the title of an essay collection, *Computational Propaganda: Political Parties, Politicians and Political Manipulation on Social Media*, eds. Samuel C. Woolley and Philip N. Howard (Oxford: Oxford University Press, 2019).

10. Uriah Marc Todoroff, interview with Brian Massumi and Erin Manning, "A Cryptoeconomy of Affect", *The New Inquiry*, 14 May 2018. https://thenewinquiry.com/a-cryptoeconomy-of-affect/ Accessed 20 May 2019.

11. Wikipedia gives this overview of "Pepe the Frog's" life as a far-right internet meme: "During the 2016 United States presidential election the meme was connected to Donald Trump's campaign. In October 2015, Trump retweeted a Pepe representation of himself, associated with a video called "You Can't Stump the Trump (Vol. 4)". Later in the election, Roger Stone and Donald Trump Jr. posted a parody movie poster of *The Expendables* on Twitter and Instagram titled "The Deplorables", a play on Hillary Clinton's controversial phrase "basket of deplorables", which included Pepe's face among those of members of the Trump family and other figures popular among the alt-right. Also during the election, various news organisations reported associations of the character with white nationalism and the alt-right. In May 2016, Olivia Nuzzi of *The Daily Beast* wrote that there was "an actual campaign to reclaim Pepe from normies", and that "turning Pepe into a white nationalist icon" was an explicit goal of some on the alt-right. In September 2016, an article published on Hillary Clinton's campaign website described Pepe as "a symbol associated with white supremacy" and denounced Trump's campaign for its supposed promotion of the meme." https://en.wikipedia.org/wiki/Pepe_the_Frog. Accessed 17 May 2019.

Silence=Death graphic used by ACT-UP (AIDS Coalition to Unleash Power), 1987.

contamination, toxicity, and demographic incursion. One could venture that the episteme of the meme (the *epistememe*, if you will), is essentially pandemic and bellicose.[12] The association of memes with viral consciousness and pack-herd mass violence underscores their volatility as a political medium; their susceptibility to appropriation and self-sabotage as in cases – like those found in the comics of R. Crumb – in which "the satire of racist bigotry is indistinguishable from bigotry itself."[13] This negative capability of memes notwithstanding, it is important to acknowledge their historic contribution as rallying points to activism and protest politics (think of ACT-UP's "Silence=Death" logo, or more recently, #BlackLivesMatter, a meme in itself that also built a series of movement memes out of Eric Garner's phrase "I Can't Breathe" and Trayvon Martin's hoodie; or the pro-choice movement's pink X-emblazoned sign and slogan #SexStrike: "If Our Choices Are Denied So Are Yours."

Amanda Ross-Ho, ***Untitled Crisis Actor (hurts as much as you can imagine, although you do not have to be crying to feel this)***, 2019.

The psychedelic, sexual, and satirical stylings of cartoonist R. Crumb.

Memes assume weird, hybrid forms both in and beyond platform politics. In aesthetics and creative practice they figure prominently in "the New Weird", a genre between fantasy and horror in speculative fiction associated with writers like H.P. Lovecraft, China Miéville and Tom McCarthy. Weird objects, according to McCarthy, are protean and formless. In his 2015 novel *Satin Island*, an oil-spill becomes an example of the Weird: a dark substance, a primeval ooze, a terrestrial ink, it presents a script written by a nonhuman (the Earth) that remains mystifyingly illegible.[14] Mikhail Gorbachev's birthmark, sometimes referred to as a "port-wine stain", exerts much the same fascination. It appears as a meme that emblematises the atmosphere of fin-de-Cold War "crazy" in Don DeLillo's 1997 novel *Underworld*:[15]

12.
See Angela Nagle, *Kill All Normies: the online culture wars from Tumblr and 4chan to the alt-right and Trump* (Washington: Zero Books, 2017). To make the point about the escalation of meme warfare Nagle asks us to compare the age of innocence when the Obama campaign circulated the HOPE meme by artist Shepard Fairey, with the "irreverent mainstream-baffling meme culture during the last race, in which the Bernie's Dank Meme Stash Facebook page and The Donald subreddit defined the tone of the race for a young and newly politicized generation, with the mainstream media desperately trying to catch up with a subcultural in-joke style to suit two emergent anti-establishment waves of the right and left. Writers like Manuel Castells and numerous commentators in *The Wired* told us of the coming of a networked society, in which old hierarchical models of business and culture would be replaced by the wisdom of crowds, the swarm, the hive mind, citizen journalism and user-generated content. They got their wish, but it's not quite the utopian vision they were hoping for." pp. 8–9.

13.
Tanner Tafelski, "The Knotty Legacy of *Weirdo*, R. Crumb's Underground Comix Magazine" in *Hyperallergic*, 14 June 2019.

14.
See Tom McCarthy and Elvia Wilke, "Just Fucking Weird", 28 March 2019, at the Haus der Kulturen der Welt, Berlin. https://www.hkw.de/en/programm/projekte/veranstaltung/p_149683.php. Accessed 10 May 2019.

15.
DeLillo's parody of paranoid over-reading was the harbinger of post-online "crazy" and 4chan bullying. The players range, as Angela Nagle's snapshot indicates, across Mencius Moldbug's "The Cathedral", Nick Land's "Dark Enlightenment", and "Peter Theil's idea to create a separate state off the coast of the US – and rightest elite applications to transhumanism." Angela Nagle, *Kill All Normies*, op. cit., p. 17.

#SEX STRIKE
IF OUR CHOICES ARE DENIED, SO ARE YOURS.

#SEXSTRIKE, a viral movement for women's reproductive rights proposed by actress Alyssa Milano.

BLACK LIVES MATTER
Not a Riot!

Black Lives Matter rally in Union Square, New York, – in solidarity with protests in Baltimore, 2015.

'You should train an eye on the mark on this Gorbachev's head, to see if it changes shape.'
'Changes shape? It's always been there.'
'You know this?'
'What, you think it recently appeared?'
'You know this? It's always been there?'
'It's a birthmark,' Brian said.
'Excuse me but that's the official biography. I'll tell you what I think. I think if I had a sensitive government job I would be photographing Gorbachev from outer space every minute of the day that he's not wearing a hat to check the shape of the birthmark if it's changing. Because it's Latvia right now. But it could be Siberia in the morning, where they're emptying out their jails.'[16]

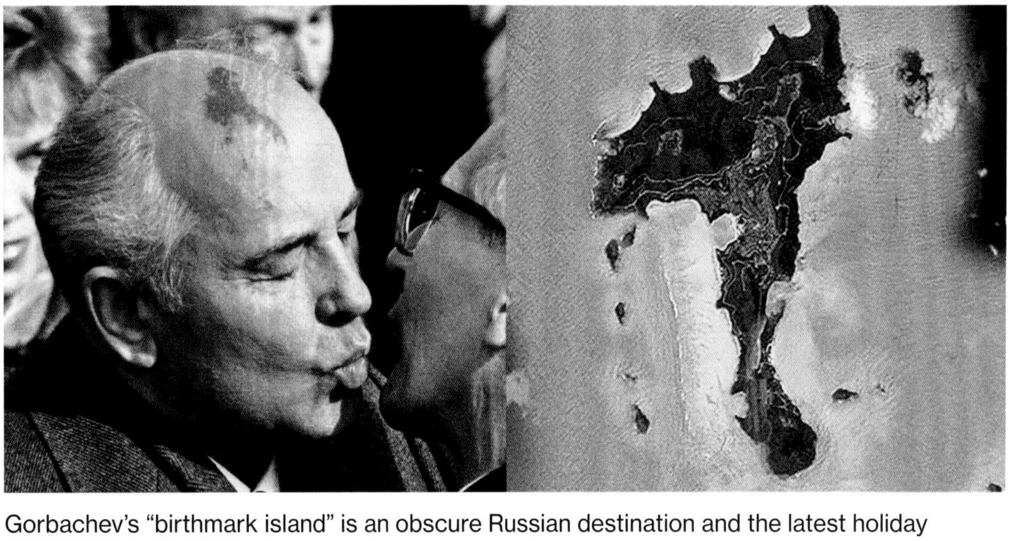

Gorbachev's "birthmark island" is an obscure Russian destination and the latest holiday phenomenon known as the "shapecation".

16.
Don DeLillo, *Underworld* (New York: Scribner, 1997), p. 181.

A meme popular with U.S. soldiers during the Second World War. Servicemen drew the figure on walls wherever they were stationed.

Flash forward to the present and you realise how this obsession has metastasized. A headline from 2019 reads, "Tourists head to 'Gorbachev birthmark' archipelago". The article explains: "An obscure Russian destination is the latest in a new holiday phenomenon known as the 'shapecation'." The reference is to Darak Aprel in northeast Russia off the Siberian coast. Tourists requesting to see "the birthmark islands" eventually prompted Russian tour operators to make it a destination spot. Here we have a triple-punch meme: the birthmark itself, "birthmark tourism", and a news item that is stranger than fiction.

Gorbachev's birthmark, like the oil-spill, is a pictogram or "crypto-concept" belonging to a larger crypto-currency of the mind. Jean Laplanche coined "crypto-concept" to designate that which "goes astray" between material and subjective reality, fact and fantasy.[17] It is what concepts lean on, are propped up by (like a subliminal subfloor), and remain oblivious of even as they quote and repeat them. One of Slavoj Žižek's "old joke[s] from Socialist times about a Yugoslav politician on a visit to Germany" says it best: "When his train passes a city, he asks his guide: 'What city is this?' The guide replies: 'Baden-Baden'. The politician snaps back: 'I'm not an idiot – you don't have to tell me twice!"[18] What's memic here is not only the repetition-effect of "Baden-Baden" or the fact that it is already a "Žižek joke" meme, but also the "I'm not an idiot" idiocy, with its affirmation of insistent obtuseness. Roland Barthes identified obtuseness (*l'obtus*) with "third meaning", using the example of the shower of gold raining

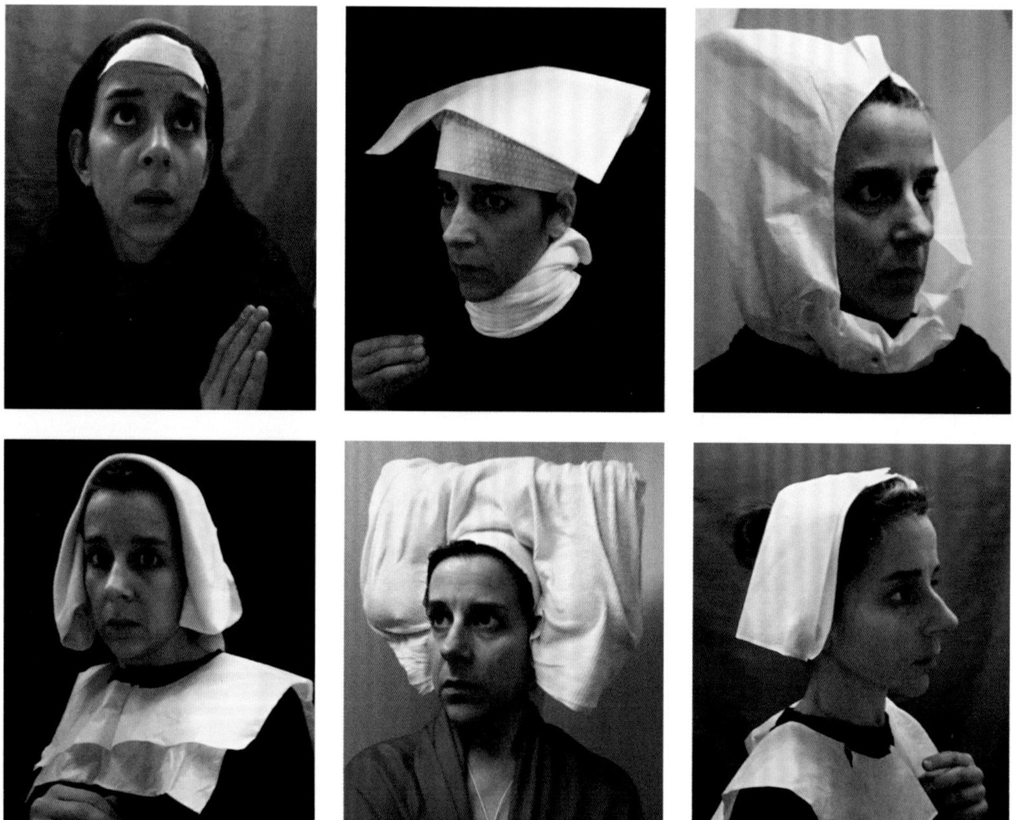

Nina Katchadourian, ***Lavatory Self-Portrait in the Flemish Style # 6, # 19, # 1, # 3, # 8***, and ***# 4***, from *Seat Assignment*, 2010–ongoing (clockwise from top left).

17.
Jean Laplanche, "The So-Called 'Death Drive': A Sexual Drive", *British Journal of Psychotherapy* 20:4 (2004), p. 458.

18.
Slavoj Žižek, *Žižek's Jokes* (Cambridge, MA: MIT Press, 2014), p. 12.

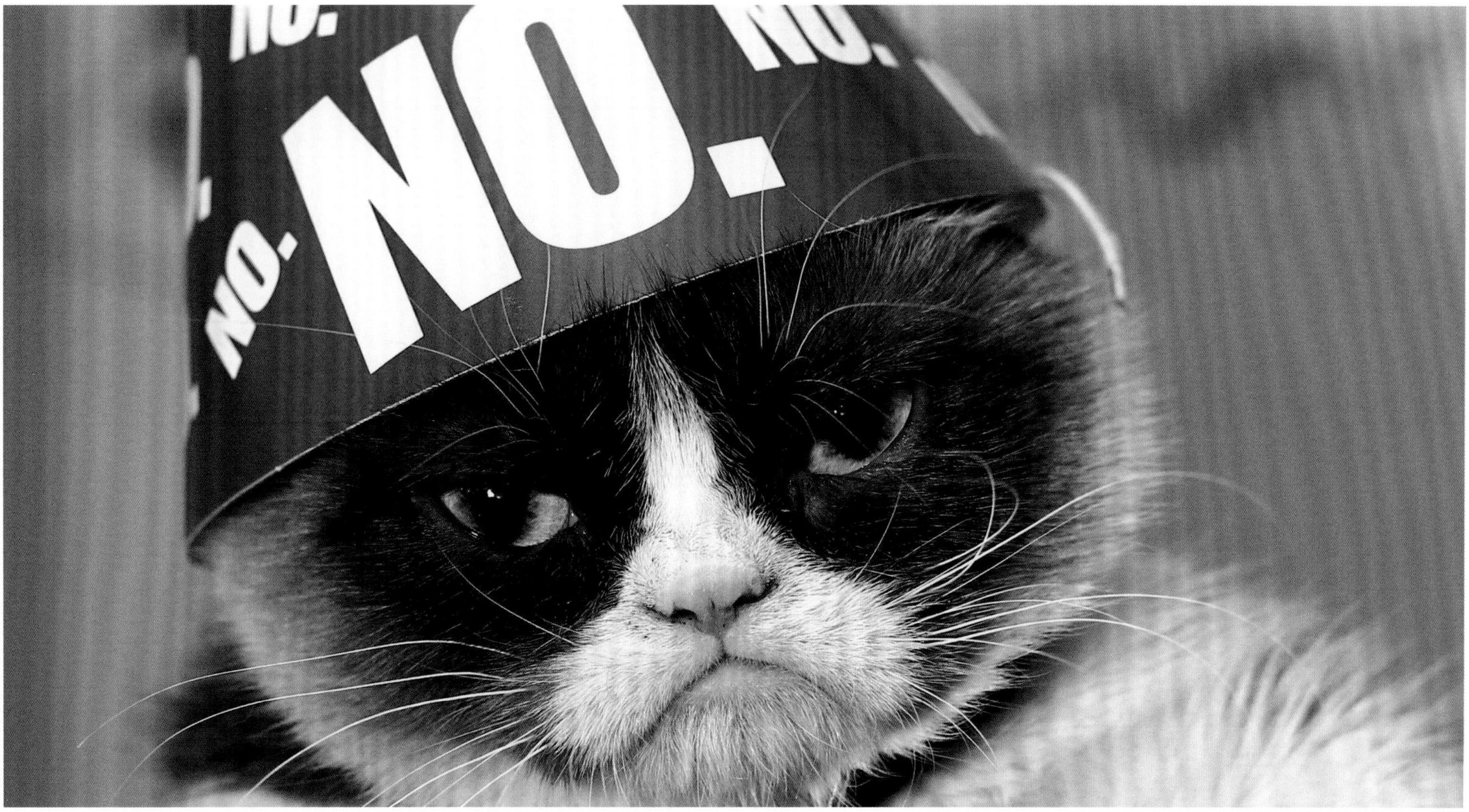

The ever-popular meme cat Tardar Sauce (aka Grumpy Cat).

down on the Tsar's head in Einstein's film *Ivan the Terrible*. Here, the historical symbolism of the gold is easy enough to decode, but there is something extra that remains harder to unravel; an "erratic, obstinate" factor, something "trivial, futile, false, pastiche."[19] Third meaning, Barthes specified, is third-order mimesis; "meme-etic" inasmuch as it is an accessory to the copy of the referential motif.

Crypto-conceptuality and obtuseness are identifying traits of memes, no matter the packaging they come in: acronyms, logos, GIFs, captchas, emojis, random phrases, aphorisms, tunes, kinky or bad fashion, "crazy shit", and tags: "Kilroy Was Here", "Frodo Lives", "Know da wae",[20] "Hamster Dance", "Scumbag Steve", "Ermagerd", "Alex from Target", "Red Slime", and "Grumpy Cat". It is this obtuseness – this ignorance of why they become memes – that comes into focus when trying to fathom what gives them lift-off. Why do certain examples of weak messaging, or random categories start to "trend"? Even witty artist memes give off some aura of bafflement about the fact of their becoming memes. Nina Katchadourian, for instance, claims that she could never have anticipated that her series *Lavatory Portraits in the Flemish Style* would go viral. Memes, then, are already born in scare-quotes, citing their own obtuseness, their indifference to the sufficient cause of their reproducibility, their status as cognitive perplex. It is this queer aspect of memes that may account, at least in part, for their prominence in feminist, queer, and artistic practice. Pre-internet, feminist artist Mary Kelly created a leather jacket meme of female masochism in her project *Interim*, Lutz Bacher memed Jane Fonda's weirdness, and Jenny Holzer fabricated a feminist self-defence meme, building off Marshall

19. Roland Barthes, "Le troisième sens", *L'obvie et l'obtus* (Paris: Seuil, 1982), p. 46.

20. For a fairly complete seminar on the genesis of the Ugandan Knuckle meme, see: https://www.youtube.com/watch?v=hVFTD-QZwMo The *Urban Dictionary* resumes its history as follows: "Possibly the January 2018 Meme of the Month, 'Do you know da wae' has taken the world by storm. Many brave, Ugandan Warriors formed by a group of Knuckles, which is a Sonic character, follow around people on VRChat, asking if they know the way. They find queens to follow, and if they find a false queen, they make spit sounds. If they find a real queen, they click their tongues to show that they are the queen's followers. This random craze is funny because of how random it is, and many people do not seem to laugh at this, usually people who are not true meme artists.

Example 1:
Warrior 1: Do you know da wae?
Anime girl: What?
Warrior 2: SHE DOES NOT KNOW DA WAE SPIT ON HER SPIT MY BROTHAS
Warrior 3: Give no mercy, for this false queen is a poser" https://www.urbandictionary.com/define.php?term=Do%20you%20know%20da%20wae. Accessed 17 June 2019.

Invitation to the feminist internet culture exhibition ***By Any Memes Necessary*** at Junior High Gallery, Los Angeles, curated by Mo Johnson (ka5sh).

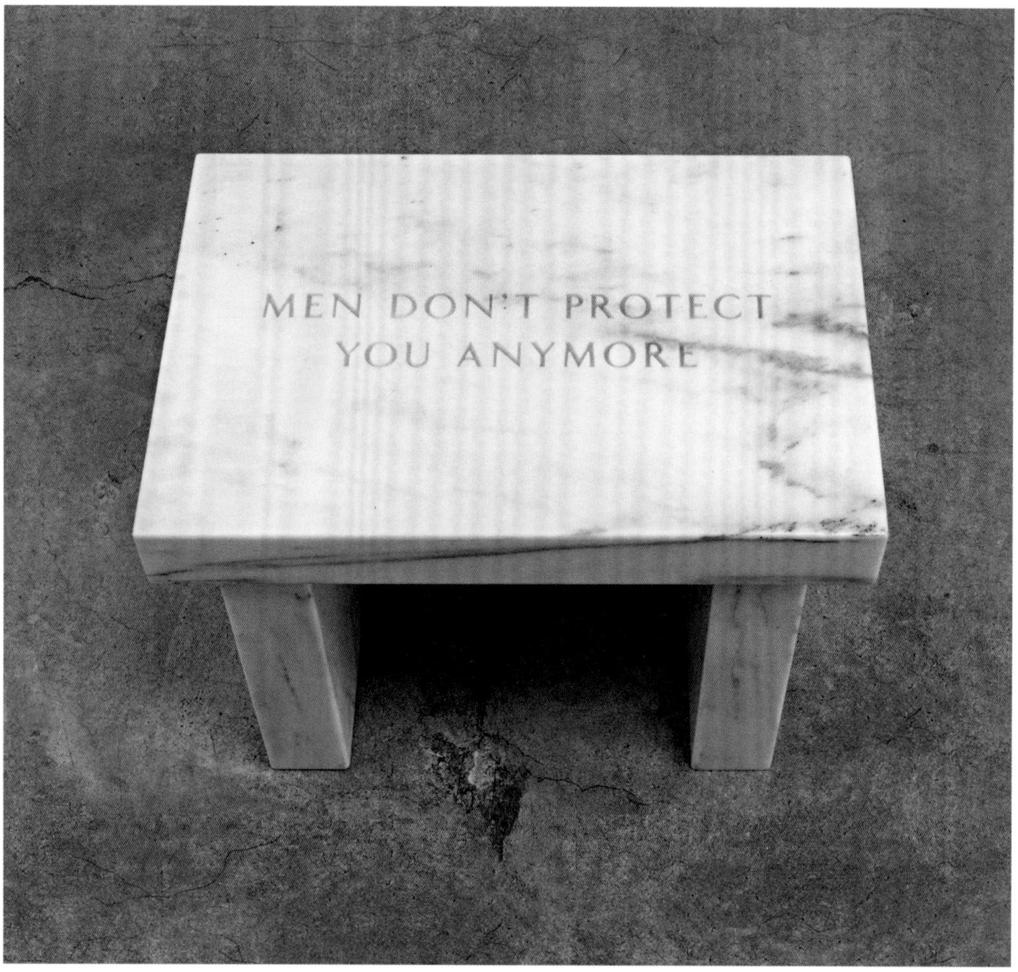

Jenny Holzer, ***The Survival Series: Men don't protect ...***, 2006.

McLuhan's notion that "the medium is the message". Post-internet, queer and feminist artists have embraced the meme as medium, as the recent exhibit *By Any Memes Necessary* attests.[21]

In their one-linerism,[22] in their association with a production process that is "back office" (largely hidden from view, and in that respect the antithesis of assembly politics), in their reliance on the short attention span and the ephemeral, virtual environments of Facebook, Twitter, and Instagram (themselves meme trademarks), and in their complicity with the art of the stupid joke (think *Žižek's Jokes*, a book whose philosophy-nerd subtitle, *Did you hear the one about Hegel and negation?* alerts readers to the lameness of philosophy and prepares them for a joke at their own expense), memes lend themselves to being dismissed as frivolous bad puns or excoriated as units of capitalist branding and rebranding.[23] It seems incontestable that internet memes flow out of a commercially-driven economy of social media, and that they increasingly populate what used to be quaintly known as "the public sphere" with a profit-harvesting avalanche of prompts, screengrabs, tweets, conspiracy theories, deepfake videos, and hoaxes. Memes are willing agents of the trollfarm, helped along by the political brands of Donald Trump, Vladimir Putin, Matteo Salvini, Jair Bolsonaro, Geert Wilders, Benjamin Netanyahu, Victor Orbán, Marine Le Pen, Jörg Haider, Nigel Farage, Narendra Modi …

21. Mo Johnson, "By Any Memes Necessary: This Art Exhibit Takes Feminist Internet Culture from URL to IRL" in *Bust*, newsletter (May / June 2019) https://bust.com/arts/19045-meme-art-exhibit.html. Accessed 17 June 2019.

22. Slavs and Tatars, "More Phemes" in *Wripped Scripped* (Berlin: Hatje Cantz Verlag, 2018), p. 7.

23. As Liam Gillick notes, the end of the last millennium ushered in a host of memes as euphemistic fixers, "new Ancient-Greek sounding names" appearing "in ambient ambivalent spaces of exchange as a replacement for more difficult and directly contestable activities or scandals: Altria, Aga, Areva, Avaya, Aviva, Capitalia, Centrica, Consignia, and Dexia were joined by Acambis, Acordis, Altadis, Aventis, Elementis, Enodis, and Invensys. By 2001, Arthur Anderson Accounting had become Accenture and Philip Morris had rebranded itself as Altria – all in an attempt to reflect the potential of new global markets and unforeseen opportunities, carried by new names that could be associated with visual affects spinning free from concrete associations." Liam Gillick, "We Lived and Thought Like Pigs: Gilles Chatelet's Devastating Prescience". https://www.e-flux.com/journal/100/268837/we-lived-and-thought-like-pigs-gilles-chtelet-s-devastating-prescience/ Accessed 17 June 2019.

The writers Divya Dwivedi and Shaj Mohan have analysed the Modi meme from this perspective in their article "The Hoax in the Cave":

> *An oversized man (56 inches to be precise) in a cave swaddled in saffron robes posing for the cameras in a stance of catatonic freeze. Frozen men in mountain caves are consecrated with divinity in the myths of the subcontinent. This image, as with all images, captures the mode of capturing as well; that is the mode in which an image is generated is registered in the very image.*[24]

New age meditation pioneered by Modi, which involves a 5-star cave with plenty photo opportunities for the folks back home and online.

"Capturing the mode of capturing" is close to what I previously ascribed to the meme. Dwivedi and Mohan seize on this feature, along with the "camera after camera" cumulative effect that compounds the "*hypophysical* cultic power of the object in the hands of the magician-gangster."

> *This particular image of the large man in the cave comes in a series of images. In one of them, a cameraman crouching obsequiously at the feet of the overbearing saffron subject and pointing at the face making the pose was caught by another camera which was focused on the same subject from behind. The latter image which reveals the making of the image is important. It shows that a hoax in politics takes many men to invent and sustain, for politics is the responsibility of the many.*

Dissecting the logic of the parts and wholes that upholds the "hoaxiness" of the hoax, and the distributed responsibility of its production values, Dwivedi and Mohan leave us with lingering questions about how power is localised and disseminated in the vast field of micropolitics, and how, despite (or because of) their hoaxiness, memes become ascendant and sovereign even if only for a brief

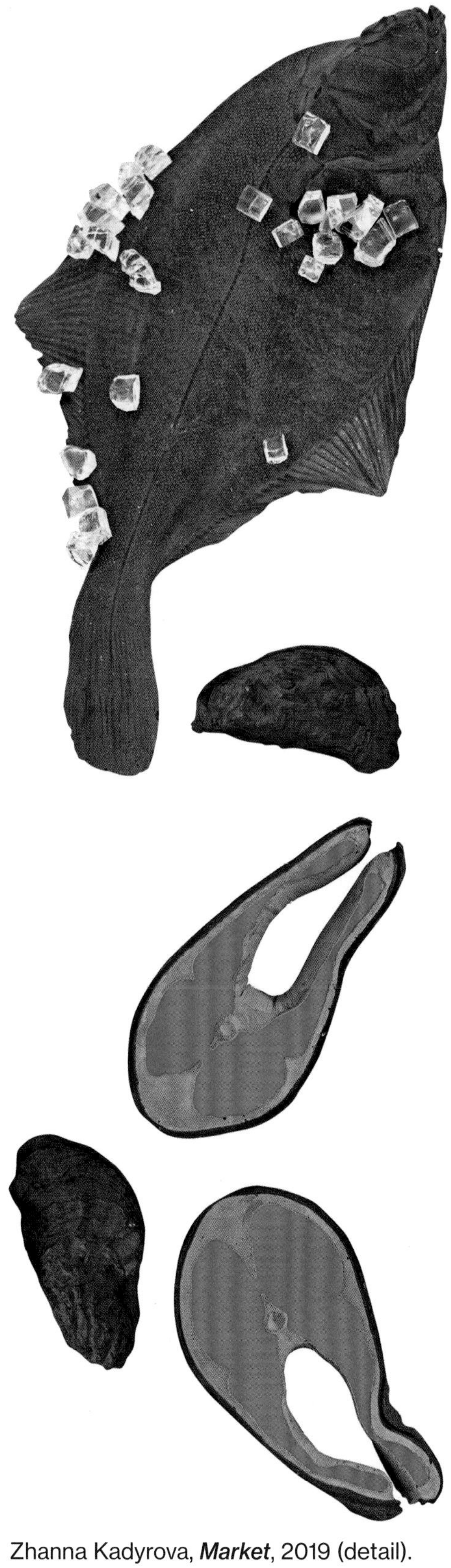

Zhanna Kadyrova, ***Market***, 2019 (detail).

24. Divya Dwivedi and Shaj Mohan, "The Hoax in the Cave", *The Wire* online. https://thewire.in/politics/narendra-modi-cave-meditation. Accessed 14 June 2019.

Nicole Wermers, ***Givers & Takers #3*** and ***#2***, 2016 (left). Nicole Wermers, ***Double Sand Table***, 2007–2018 (back). Marlie Mul, ***Puddle (Shallow Match)***, 2014 (front). Installation view at the 33rd Ljubljana Biennial of Graphic Arts, 2019.

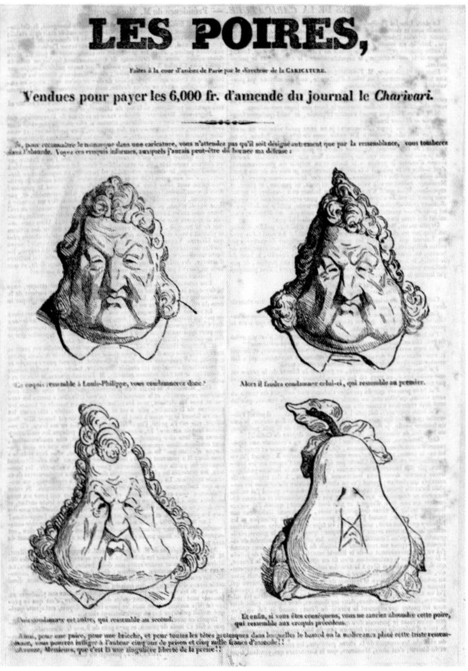

Honoré Daumier, ***Les poires*** (*The Pears*), published in *La Caricature*, 1831. The juicy fruit bears resemblance to the portly visage of King Louis-Philippe.

time: "Is this man the whole of the hoax? Is it the robe? Is it the stone idols who are legal persons in the juridical system? Is it the media? Is it in our myths which are continuous with our present? Is it our histories?" The Modi "Man in the Cave" meme, ginned up by viral circuits of "millions of followers", illustrates the way in which memes have emerged as the political technology *du jour*. There is, though, something in the obtuseness of memes along with the unstable conditions of political literacy that often makes them backfire on dictators. Dwivedi and Mohan's *exposé* of the Modi hoax itself went viral. One could say that politically speaking, meme-ology derails the authoritarian political brand as it moves, in aleatory fashion, into remote byways of audience, into greater powers of "we". It comes to resemble a certain form of comedy that, as Lauren Berlant and Sianne Ngai suggest, induces the kind of epistemological turbulence that structures of governmentality are at pains to contain or curtail:

> *Comedy isn't just an anxiogenic tableau of objects disrupted by status shifting, collapse and persistence, the disruption by difference, or a veering between the tiny and the large. Nor is it just a field of narrative expectation punctuated by the surprise of laughter or vertiginous enjoyment. It is also epistemologically troubling, drawing insecure boundaries as though it were possible to secure confidence about object ontology or the value of an 'us' versus all its others. Political cartoons, religious iconoclasm, matters of the risible are sometimes ordinary and, in some places, matters of life and death. … Comedy helps us test or figure out what it means to say 'us.' … What lines we desire or can bear.*[25]

Mobilised as a comic medium, memes test the conceptual boundaries of existential belonging and political community, and critically reboot the venerable tradition of political satire for an era of micropolitics.[26] Though they can blur the outlines of political programme by fusing the narcissism of "individual users" with outwardly directed expressions of targeted political rage, memes make political history legible and micropolitically re-programmable, in the sense of Mark Fisher's oft-quoted affirmation in *Capitalist Realism*: "The tiniest event can tear a hole in the grey curtain of reaction which has marked the horizons of possibility under capitalist realism. From a situation in which nothing can happen, suddenly anything is possible again."[27]

At their best, memes breathe new life into the art of political caricature whose history, as E.H. Gombrich and Ernst Kris elaborated in their 1938 landmark article "The Principles of Caricature", traces back to the end of the 16th-century when the mock-portraits of the Caraccis and the writing about *ritratti caricchi* (meaning "caricature" or "charge") spawned a genre of grotesque comic likeness.[28] Satire, akin to caricature, but arguably less tied down to physiognomic "tabs of identity", attained its heyday in the aftermath of the French Revolution and the July Revolution (which occasioned Philippon's wildly popular caricature of the constitutional monarch Louis-Philippe as "the Pear King").[29] Consider a typical James Gillray caricature from 1793 featuring Prime Minister William Pitt, at a moment of Britain's maximal fear of revolutionary contagion. Pitt steers a small boat named "The Constitution" with Britannia on

25.
Lauren Berlant and Sianne Ngai, eds., "Comedy Has Issues" in *Critical Inquiry* 43:2 (Winter, 2017), p. 233.

26.
In *Memes to Movements: How the World's Most Viral Media is Changing Social Protest and Power* (Boston: Beacon Press, 2019), Xiao Mina writes: "Hashtags and memes created in a context of social change often serve as micronarratives. Stop Kony. Uganda is not Spain. Chen Guangcheng will defeat Pandaman. Trayvon Martin faced systemic racism. Hoodies are powerful. Through satire and repetition, social media users are able to shape and define a narrative, and through intentional overproduction, they start arriving at narratives that have the potential to resonate more broadly." p. 75.

27.
Mark Fisher, *Capitalist Realism. Is There No Alternative?* (England: Zero Books, 2009).

28.
E.H. Gombrich and Ernst Kris, "The Principles of Caricature", *British Journal of Medical Psychology*, 17 (1938), pp. 319–342. https://gombricharchive.files.wordpress.com/2011/05/showdoc85.pdf. Accessed 17 June 2019. The authors situate the art of caricature in a Freudian field of mind play, sensory stimulus, dream-construction and affective play, noting their methodological debt to Freud in drawing on psychology as "the science of the integration of sensation, perception and desire."

29.
Ibid. The authors interpret the effect of the "Pear King" caricature through the Freudian lens of transformation and condensation. The psychic apparatus of "primary process" becomes ascendant, putting conscious logic out of action (as in a dream or the working of wit). The caricaturist capitalises on this effect, turning it consciously into a "grammar of form" that eventually culminates in Mannerist style.

board. She expresses alarm at the sight of a tricolour cockade on the summit. Three "sharks" – the prominent politicians Sheridan, Fox, and Priestly (all supporters of the French Revolution) – chase the boat, adding peril to its passage through the strait. The picture bears the caption, "The Vessel of the Constitution steered clear of the Rock of Democracy and the Whirlpool of Arbitrary Power". This caricature is didactic and hardly resembles the modern meme yet, in a prototypical way, it "phemes" the political in ways that prepare the ground for "meming" the political. Peirce gave the technical definition of a "pheme" as a sign that stands in for a whole sentence, but one could say that in the grander scheme of internet micropolitics, "pheming the political" points to an emergent "meme-caricature-satire" nexus, itself qualified by the art collective Slavs and Tatars as "the twisted nexus of politics, affect, and society at the heart of alphabet politics."[30] This alphabet politics relies on the memic (technology-enabled) potential of transliteration;[31] whose morphemes consist of historical scripts, cartographic shapes, folk art, religious icons, stamps, flags, banners, billboards, posters, portraits, publicity shots, book illustrations, adverts, cover art, political decrees, and much more.[32]

Media theorists continue to offer optimistic prognoses of the progressive political potential of meme politics. Sasha Costanza-Chock coined the expression "transmedia organizing" with reference to the way in which "social movements are becoming transmedia hubs, where new visions of society are encoded into digital texts by movement participants, then shared, aggregated, remixed and circulated ever more widely across platforms." For Costanza-Chock, "despite

James Gillray, ***Britannia between Scylla and Charybdis***, 1793.

30.
Slavs and Tatars, "Transvestite Transliteration: The Case of Uyghur versus Atatürk", Blogpost LEAP 38, 2 June 2016. "To unravel the twisted nexus of politics, affect, and society at the heart of alphabet politics, we need a full arsenal of nose-, throat-, ear-, lip- and tongue twisters." http://www.leapleapleap.com/2016/06/transvestite-transliteration-the-case-of-uyghur-versus-ataturk/. Accessed 17 June 2019.

31.
To appreciate the morpheme as unit of political caricature and source of "more memes" we might look to Slavs and Tatars' homonymic play on themes and phonemes in the section "More Phemes" in their book *Wripped Scripped*. The book presents a catalogue of translatable icons, many recording the impact of successive waves of imperial conquest, regime change, and superpositions of religion and language over the variegated territories of Eurasia (Islamic, Christian Orthodox, Persian, Ottoman, French, Russian, Chinese …). It opens with an Arcimboldo-style composition of Adam, the original man. His hair parting, nose-line, and symmetrical moustachio form a system of face-letters merged with the Arabic alphabet, spelling out the phrase "generosity of God" *fazl-i haqq*; Islam written over Christianity. In a second iteration (minus spectacles and hair) the image is captioned, as if parodying educational copy, "The eyes, nose and mustache spell 'Ali.'" Adam's visage mirrors bisected worlds and this *bi-* motif is humorously exploited to plot serial likenesses among disparate political phenomena: bisexual icons (Saint Wilgefortis in drag), Eastern Europe's attacks on Western affirmations of nonbinary sexuality, schizo-analytic objects (a pair of bisected Courrèges glasses), and cringeworthy images of women gymnasts doing the splits in front of a lascivious group of Polish officials (The caption reads: "Andrzej Duda and gender-geriatric colleagues at the 100th anniversary of Polish Independence, 10 January 2018"). Throughout, memes are created out of historic icons and political brand trademarks with the implicit (if not express) intent to enhance political literacy. Culled from the detritus of empires and revolutions, these new memes – which spell out the micropolitics of "Eurasia" while decomposing its constitutive clichés – stir up subterranean resources in the historical memory archive. As we are visually marched through the Ottoman Empire, the Eastern Bloc, the Russian steppes, the Balkans, the Iranian Revolution, and the Polish Solidarity movement, there is a crack-up of geopolitical and regional blandishments about bipolar axes of power (the "axis of evil"), East versus West, secular / non-secular dichotomies, hard lines of distinction among capitalist, socialist, and communist ideologies, and economies and binary political thinking *tout court*. See: Slavs and Tatars, "More Phemes" in *Wripped Scripped* (Berlin: Hatje Cantz Verlag, 2018), pp. 7 and 14.

32.
Hamja Ahsan's project *Shy Radicals: The Antisystemic Politics of the Militant Introvert* satirises the nexus of state government and states of affect (shyness) through a meme-friendly appropriation of authorising political documents: articles of national foundation, acts of parliament, declarations of rights, and so on. Under the proclamation "We, the Peoples of Aspergistan" a body of legislation is put forth outlawing "the global system of Extrovert-Suprematism" and decreeing a code of conduct based on Lao Tzu's dictum "the quieter you become, the more you are able to hear." If there is explicitly memic content here, it is found in the →

Flaka Haliti, ***Is it you, Joe? (Hangover)***, 2017.

Slavs and Tatars, ***Make Mongolia Great Again***, 2016.

digital inequality, the praxis of critical digital media literacy can produce subjects able to fully participate in transmedia organizing."[33] Citing this passage, Xiao Mina waxes hopefully: "Social change memes take their place in the long line of activist art and culture – from street theater to graffiti – which aim to disrupt and challenge narratives in the public space. ... Memes help us envision another world, a practice known as *prefigurative* politics ..."[34] The word "prefigurative" takes us back to René Thom's suggestive construct of *pregnance* – with its connotations of expectancy, pregnancy, and (extrapolating here), predictive processing that produces mutational hylomorphism minus the politically fore-ordained. I would concur in recognising memes as a currency of political morphogenesis that harbour the capacity to alter political landscapes at the level of the micro-physics of power, but would caution against reading too much hope into their "platform cooperativism", their enhanced technology of political messaging, or their renewal of graffiti and street art. I would look instead to their potential as a medium of alphabet politics reliant on the raw material and skill sets of political transliteration and grounded in satire. The art of political satire depends on political literacies attuned to the fine grain of diplomatic and parliamentary manoeuvring, espionage, the geopolitical stakes of the Great Game, the foibles and indiscretions of political actors, backroom scandals and scams, informal politics and information-trafficking, and infrastructures of distributed responsibility that leave a significant though often barely perceptible cognitive imprint on the "what happens" of the political everyday. This mysterious "what happens" is co-extensive with the obtuseness of all memes, which is to say with their crypto-conceptual propping, leaning and guideposting in the unseen spheres of political influence.

Overtly satirical memes abridge past and future political technologies and help recover a sense of politics as *métier*, as professional praxis, as a form of

prescriptive hand and body language diagrams coded as "the new lexicon of democracy." We read: "All democratic decisions and motions are to be negotiated via a series of hand and body gestures to arrive at a consensus. Whilst previous non-hierarchical social movements had experimented with moving beyond the language of applause and booing with what we call 'wiggly hands' (also known by them as 'up twinkles' or 'spirit fingers'), the Shy Radicals movement nevertheless identify 'wiggly hands' as representing a serious democratic deficit." See: Hamja Ahsan, *Shy Radicals: The Antisystemic Politics of the Militant Introvert* (London: Book Works 2019), pp. 14, 39–40 respectively.

33. Sasha Costanza-Chock, *Out of the Shadows, Into the Streets!* (Cambridge, MA: MIT Press, 2014), p. 195, as cited by Xiao Mina, in *Memes to Movements. How the World's Most Viral Media is Changing Social Protest and Power*, op. cit., p. 76.

34. Xiao Mina, *Memes to Movements. How the World's Most Viral Media is Changing Social Protest and Power*, op. cit., pp. 76–77.

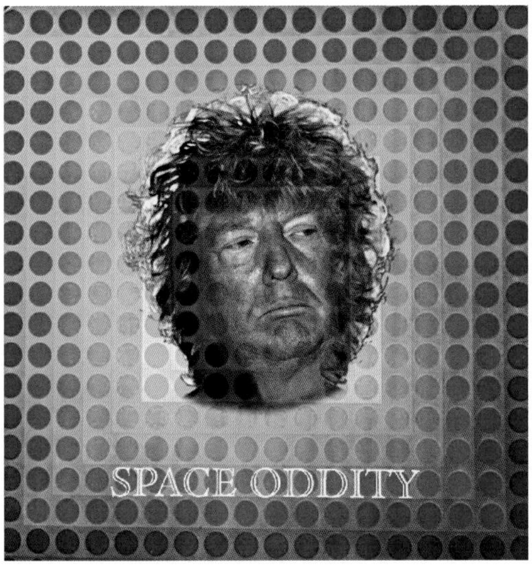

Silvia Kolbowski, ***Ground Control to Major Trump***, 2018.

what Arne de Boever calls "plastic sovereignty" that retains "sovereignty's positive accomplishments."[35] These include the skills of the professional organiser; non-vertical axes of agency; autopoeic transformation over and against 'neoliberal flexibility", and a "new experience of language."[36] Pushing further, one could say that satirical memes – in all their obtuseness – enable us to re-learn: they become part of a re-education plan in reading (and changing) politics. By way of example, consider Silvia Kolbowski's Trump-David Bowie meme (captioned "Ground Control to Major Trump"), in which we obtain a screen-capture of the psychic shape of power. The mind-meld of these iconic figures, one a reckless oligarch, the other a revered pop idol, produces a disturbing emblem of rage and desire. It morphs according to the welter of what is at hand, including the drives and affects floating up from the unconscious. Kolbowski intimates that we get the politicians we meme for. What, she queries, "if Trump were actually himself a phantasm projected by his 'base,' rather than his base being an inherently evil group to which he plays? What if he is an effect – a hologram – of their rage?"[37] Whether we approach memes as holograms of partisan affect or forms of satire that undercut authoritarian rule, one thing seems clear: as a crypto-currency of micropolitics, satirical memes offer instruction in the becoming-historical of what Gombrich and Kris called a "grammar of form".[38] Memic caricature has the capacity to stigmatise its targeted subject, but it also traces the outlines of the abuse of power, etching its occurrence on historical memory, transmitting it epigenetically as historical form and idea. As Gombrich and Kris noted (and it is impossible at the present pass not to have Trump in mind): "If the caricature fits the victim really is transformed in our eyes. We learn through the artist to see him as a caricature. He is not only mocked or unmasked, but actually changed. He carries the caricature with him through his life and even through history."[39]

35. Arne de Boever, *Plastic Sovereignties: Agamben and the Politics of Aesthetics* (Edinburgh: Edinburgh University Press, 2016), p. 23.

36. Ibid., p. 28.

37. Silvia Kolbowski, "Ground Control to Major Trump", Silviakolbowskiblog, 7 May 2018. https://silviakolbowskiblog.com/2018/05/07/ground-control-to-major-trump/ Accessed 17 June 2019.

38. E.H. Gombrich and Ernst Kris, "The Principles of Caricature", op. cit.

39. Ibid.

BUTALCI

Butalci are humorous folk characters created by Fran Milčinski (1867–1932), appearing in his satirical short stories. Milčinski worked for most of his life as a lawyer and judge for a juvenile court. This material inspired his later fictional work, which he began writing after the birth of his children. His satirical folk tales were first published in 1917 in *The Brigand Mataj and other Slovene Tales*, and later posthumously collected in a volume entitled *Butalci* in 1949. Milčinski created the Butalci as residents of the fictional town of Butale, satirised as bumbling dullards who bicker over small-town disputes and are forever in competition with residents from the neighbouring village of Tepanje. They are said to "lack for nothing, only sense." Milčinski's short stories have been made into children's books, plays, and feature in carnival celebrations throughout Slovenia. Through intelligent satire and astute witticisms, Milčinski crafted celebrated stories that serve as timeless and cautionary tales about the consequences of ignorance, miscommunication, and in-fighting.

Honza Zamojski, ***The Gathering and The Meeting***, 2019. Installation view at the 33rd Ljubljana Biennial of Graphic Arts, 2019.

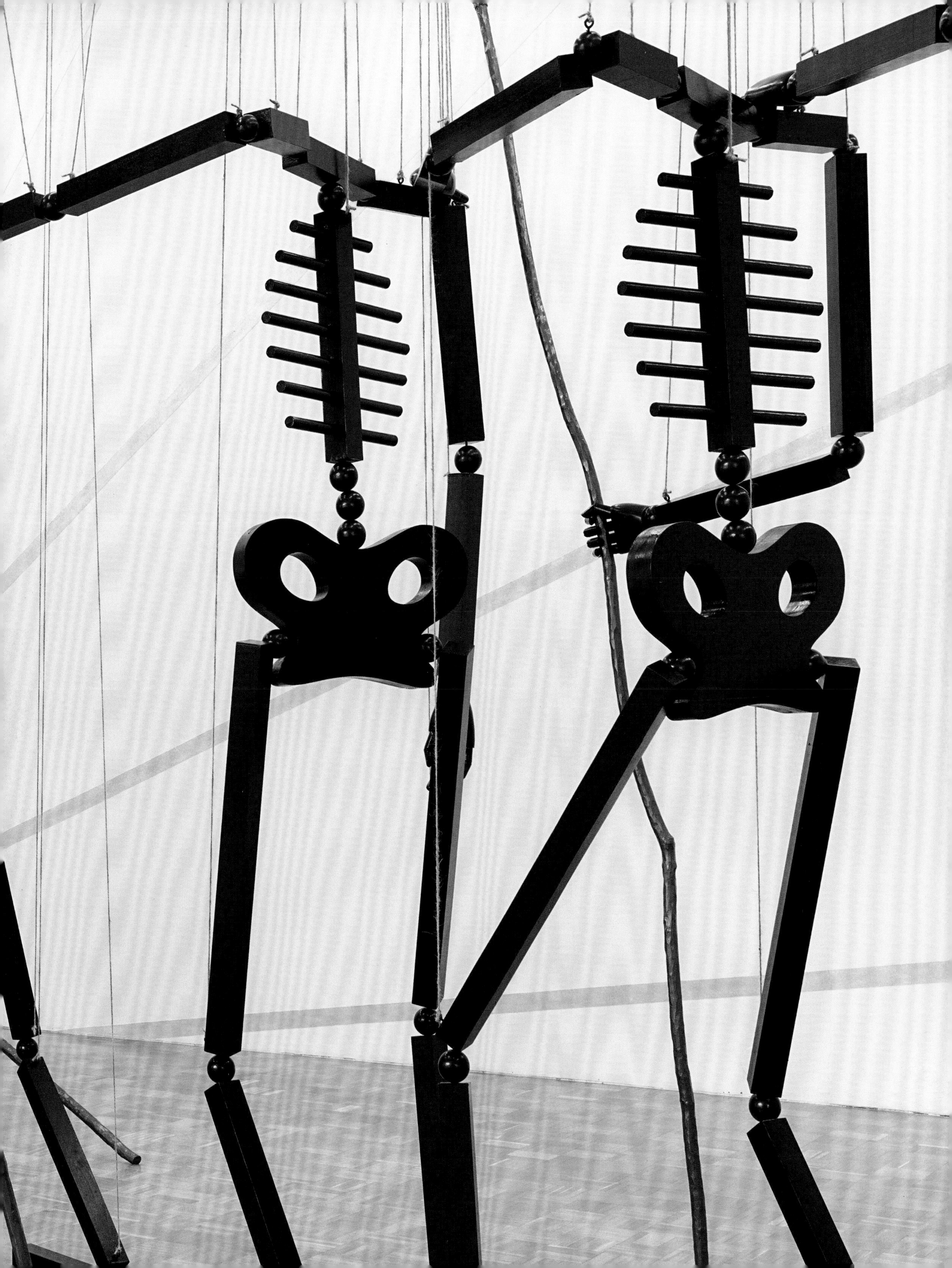

All installation views of the 33rd Ljubljana Biennial of Graphic Arts are photographed by Jaka Babnik. MGLC archive.

p. 5
- MGLC archive, courtesy: Lin May Saeed, Jacky Strenz Frankfurt am Main, Nicolas Krupp, Basel
- Studio Tatuażu Manta, pinterest.ca

p. 6
- MGLC archive, courtesy: Cevdet Erek and AKINCI, Amsterdam
- UNICEF, *I dream of peace*, (New York: HarperCollins Publishers, Inc., 1994)

p. 7
- MGLC archive

p. 8
- MGLC archive, photo: Urška Boljkovac
- mutualart.com

p. 9
- courtesy: the archive of the Museum of Puppetry of the Ljubljana Puppet Theatre, photo: Zala Kalan
- courtesy: National and University Library archive, Ljubljana
- friday.az
- simplicissimus.info

p. 10
- thepublicsradio.org, photo: Darko Bandic
- photo: REUTERS / Valentyn Ogirenko

p. 14
- MGLC archive, courtesy: the Top Lista Nadrealista cast and creators

p. 17
- wikimedia.org

p. 18
- Fran Levstik, *Martin Krpan z Vrha*, (Ljubljana: Mladinska knjiga, 1954). Courtesy: Mladinska knjiga Publishing House and Vanda Vremšak Richter.
- courtesy: Marlie Mul and Croy Nielsen

p. 19
- wikimedia.org
- courtesy: Salinen Prosol d.o.o, Ljubljana

p. 20
- courtesy: National Gallery of Slovenia, photo: Bojan Salaj
- Fran Levstik, *Martin Krpan* (Ljubljana: Mladinska knjiga, 2017). Courtesy: Mladinska knjiga Publishing House and Uroš Bučar.

p. 21
- courtesy: Zavod Strip art, Ljubljana
- hellenicaworld.com

p. 22
- onb.ac.at
- nga.gov

p. 23
- courtesy: Tala Madani and Pilar Corrias, London
- politika.rs
- sutori.com

p. 24
- MGLC archive, courtesy: the Top Lista Nadrealista cast and creators

p. 25
- MGLC archive, courtesy: Lawrence Abu Hamdan

pp. 26–27
- MGLC archive, courtesy: Endre Tot

p. 28
- MGLC archive, courtesy: Honza Zamojski, Drei, Cologne

p. 29
- courtesy: Comedy Central
- Fran Levstik, Martin Krpan (Ljubljana: Mladinska knjiga, 2017). Courtesy: Mladinska knjiga Publishing House and Uroš Bučar.
- fanaru.com

p. 30
- Fran Levstik, *Martin Krpan z Vrha*, (Ljubljana: Mladinska knjiga, 1954). Courtesy: Mladinska knjiga Publishing House and Vanda Vremšak Richter.
- MGLC archive, courtesy: Woody de Othello and Jessica Silverman Gallery, San Francisco

p. 31
- courtesy: James McCauley / REX / Shutterstock
- MGLC archive, courtesy: Martina Vacheva and Sariev Contemporary

p. 32
- MGLC archive, courtesy: Martina Vacheva and Sariev Contemporary

p. 33
- MGLC archive

pp. 34–35
- Eduard Fuchs (dir.), *Süddeutscher Postillon: Politisch-Satirisches Arbeiterblatt* (*The South German Carriage Driver: Political-Satirical Worker's Newspaper*), biweekly journal (Munich: M. Ernst, 1899).

p. 36
- Henry Wessells, *Donald Trump The Magazine of Poetry*, (New Jersey: Temporary Culture, 2016).

p. 37
- Michael Myers, *Impeach Nixon*, linocut printed bumpersticker (San Francisco: Hermes Free Press, ca. 1972).

pp. 38–40
- Eduard Fuchs, *Die Weiberherrschaft in the Geschichte der Menschheit* (*Women Domination in the History of Humanity*), Vol. 3 (Munich: Albert Langen, 1913).

p. 41
- wikimedia.org

p. 42
- courtesy: Hamja Ahsan

p. 43
- third edition 2019, 11.3 × 17.5, 168 pages, softcover, published by Book Works, London, in 2017 as part of Common Objectives, courtesy: Hamja Ahsan

p. 44
- MGLC archive, photo: Urška Boljkovac, courtesy: Hamja Ahsan

p. 45
- courtesy: Clarissa Thieme

p. 46
- archive.balkaninsight.com, courtesy: Leo Nikolic

p. 47
- John Lamm, *DeLorean: Stainless Steel Illusion* (Newport: Newport Press, 1983).
- courtesy: Trio Sarajevo
- William J. Clinton Presidential Library

p. 48
- canadianaci.ca
- youtube.com

p. 49
- courtesy and photo: Paul Chan, Creative Time and Greene Naftali, New York

pp. 50–51
- MGLC archive, courtesy: Pablo Bronstein

p. 52
- relics-rarities.com
- AP images, photo: Peter Northall

p. 53
- wikimedia.org
- courtesy: Gary Knight, VII and Redux

p. 54
- courtesy: Stane Jagodič
- MGLC archive, courtesy: Sachiko Kazama, and MUJIN-TO Production

p. 55
- theonion.com

pp. 56–57
- MGLC archive, courtesy: Lawrence Abu Hamdan

p. 58
- wikimedia.org

p. 59
- wikimedia.org
- courtesy: Sarajevo Center for Contemporary Art, photo: Lejla Hodžić

p. 60
- youtube.com
- Angelos Baš, ed., *Slovensko ljudsko izročilo: pregled etnologije Slovencev* (Cankarjeva založba, 1980). Photo: Niko Kuret, 26. 9. 1954, Bukovci 113, Puppeteer Franc Šmigoc, farmer, shoemaker and musician, with the puppets known as "lilek". Archive of the Institute of Slovenian Ethnology SRC SASA. Courtesy: ISE SRC SASA.

p. 62
- *Toufigh Satirical Journal*, 9 April, 1953
- *Toufigh Satirical Journal*, 22 August, 1962

p. 63
- *Ahangar*, 1 April 1979
- *Ahangar*, 2 April 1979

p. 64
- *Ahangar*, 13 July 1979
- *Ahangar*, 6 May 1979

p. 65
- *Ahangar*, 1 April 1979
- *Ahangar*, 6 May 1979

p. 66
- instagram.com/iran_art_meme/

p. 67
- *Scharmgah*, 26 May 2016
- twitter.com/humansoflateje

p. 68
- *Ahangar*, 14 July 1979
- *Ahangar*, 13 July 1979

pp. 69–72
- courtesy: Alenka Pirman & KULA

p. 73
- National Library of Poland

p. 74
- photo: Kevin Cummins
- courtesy: Fritz Brinckmann / Faceland
- thewindow.barneys.com

p. 75
- rbtoday.ru, Misha Buster archive
- KP archive

p. 76
- courtesy: Society for Theoretical Psychoanalysis archive
- wikimedia.org

p. 77
- Archiv der Jugendkulturen e.v.

p. 78
- wikimedia.org
- Anna Dąbrowska-Lyons, *Polski punk 1978–1982* (Warsaw: Agencja Promocyjno-Wydawnicza "ADA", 1999).
- Paweł Konjo Konnak, *Explozja Zlewu*, Vol. 1 (Warsaw: Narodowe Centrum Kultury, 2016).

p. 79
- Piotr Rypson archive
- mikes-szmata.bandcamp.com

p. 80
- Czesław Bielecki, Jan Krzysztof Kelus and Urszula Sikorska, *Mały Konspirator* (Wrocław: Agencja Informacyjna Solidarności Walczącej, 1983; reprinted from: Warsaw: CDN, 1983).
  – Folwark zwierzęcy, Komiks wg Orwella (*Animal Farm. Comics After Orwell*). (Warsaw: Gilosz & Azyl [Słowo], 1985).

p. 81
- vons.cz/vokno-en

pp. 82–83
- MGLC archive, courtesy: KRIWET and BQ Berlin

p. 84
- courtesy: Anna Uddenberg and Kraupa-Tuskany Zeidler, Berlin
- wikimedia.org

p. 85
- database.unearthingthemusic.eu

p. 86
- Muzeum Narodowe w Warszawie

p. 87
- courtesy: László Rajk

p. 88
- MGLC archive, courtesy: Giorgi Xaniashvili

p. 89
- Lesbian Library and Archive at ŠKUC LL, Ljubljana
- courtesy: Martine Gutierrez and Ryan Lee, New York

p. 90
- MGLC archive, courtesy: XIYADIE and NOME gallery, Berlin

p. 91
- bukowskis.com
- calvertjournal.com

p. 92
- MGLC archive, courtesy: Dozie Kanu and Salon 94 Design
- falajf.si. Cerknica Carnival, 2019, photo: Falajfl.

p. 93
- MGLC archive, photo: Urška Boljkovac

pp. 94–96
- courtesy: Augustin Maurs

p. 98
- katab.asia
- courtesy: Metahaven

p. 99
- illustration by Elsa El Haïby / Slavs and Tatars

p. 100
- illustration by Matt Furie
- illustration by Beth Neville
- washingtonpost.com

p. 101
- twitter.com

p. 102
- forestdweller18285.blogspot.com
- MGLC archive, courtesy: Amanda Ross-Ho and Mary Mary, Glasgow

p. 103
- wikimedia.org
- ventmil.com
- wikimedia.org
- avax.news

p. 104
- wikimedia.org
- courtesy: Nina Katchadourian, Catharine Clark Gallery, San Francisco, and Pace Gallery, New York.

p. 105
- wallpaperzen.org

p. 106
- bust.com
- sothebys.com

p. 107
- the-uma.org
- MGLC archive, courtesy: Zhanna Kadyrova and GALLERIA CONTINUA, San Gimignano, Beijing, Les Moulins, Havana

pp. 108–109
- MGLC archive, courtesy: Nicole Wermers, Herald St., London; Jessica Silverman Gallery, San Francisco; Produzentengalerie Hamburg; and Tanya Bonakdar Gallery, New York

p. 110
- wikimedia.org

p. 111
- britishmuseum.org

p. 112
- courtesy: Flaka Haliti and LamdaLamdaLamda

p. 113
- silviakolbowskiblog.com
- Fran Milčinski, *Butalci* (Ljubljana: Mladinska knjiga, 2017), illustrated by Peter Škerl. Courtesy: Mladinska knjiga Publishing House and Peter Škerl.

pp. 114–115
- MGLC archive, courtesy: Honza Zamojski and Drei, Cologne

p. 120
- MGLC archive, courtesy: Amanda Ross-Ho and Mary Mary, Glasgow

Back cover
- courtesy: National Gallery of Slovenia, photo: Bojan Salaj

COLOPHON

CRACK UP – CRACK DOWN

Editors
M. Constantine, Slavs and Tatars
Publication Manager
Asya Yaghmurian
Graphic Design and Typesetting
Stan de Natris / Slavs and Tatars
Illustrations
Nejc Prah
Design Assistance
Elsa El Haïby / Slavs and Tatars
Publication Coordinator and
Image Research Assistant
Vesna Česen Rošker
Image Research
Mara Goldwyn, Slavs and Tatars
Copy Editing
Paul Steed
Proofreading
Josephine Baker-Heaslip
Slovene-to-English Translation
Maja Lovrenov
Lithography
Tadeusz Mirosz

Accompanying *Crack Up - Crack Down*,
the exhibition of the 33rd Ljubljana Biennial
of Graphic Arts
MGLC – International Centre
of Graphic Arts
Grad Tivoli, Pod turnom 3,
Ljubljana, Slovenia
7 June–29 September 2019

Curator
Slavs and Tatars
Assistant Curator
Asya Yaghmurian
Exhibition Design
Stan de Natris / Slavs and Tatars
Exhibition Design Assistance
Kaiu Meiner, Sophia Msaoubi /
Slavs and Tatars
Identity Design
Nejc Prah
Director
Nevenka Šivavec
Assistant Director
Yasmín Martín Vodopivec
Coordinator
Božidar Zrinski
Public Programme
Lili Šturm, Asya Yaghmurian,
Slavs and Tatars

Participating Artists and Contributors
Lawrence Abu Hamdan
Hamja Ahsan
Emily Apter
Pablo Bronstein
Dragoș Cristian
Cevdet Erek
Woody De Othello
Arthur Fournier & Raphael Koenig
Martine Gutierrez
Flaka Haliti
Stane Jagodič
Zhanna Kadyrova
Dozie Kanu
KRIWET
Sachiko Kazama
Ella Kruglyanskaya
Tala Madani
Augustin Maurs
Metahaven
Marlie Mul
Marina Orsag
Alenka Pirman & KULA
Boštjan Gorenc - Pižama
Amanda Ross-Ho
Lin May Saeed
Mohammad Salemy
Vid Simoniti
Hinko Smrekar
Top Lista Nadrealista
Endre Tot
Anna Uddenberg
Martina Vacheva
Pavlo Voytovich
Nicole Wermers
Anja Wutej
Giorgi Xaniashvili
XIYADIE
Honza Zamojski

Slavs and Tatars would like to thank
Jaka Babnik
Zdenka Badovinac
Ajdin Bašić
Alina Bliumis
Urška Boljkovac
Fritz Brinckmann
Uroš Bučar
Book Works
Alexander Burenkov and Strelka
Institute for Media Architecture
and Design
Hera Chan
Clementine Deliss
Zenit Đozić
Branko Đurić
Amanda Flores
Greene Naftali Gallery
Nathalie Hoyos, Rainald Schumacher
and Art Collection Telekom
Barbara Jaki
Ana Janevski
Jessica Silverman Gallery
Jure Kirbiš
Gal Kirn
Anastasia Marukhina
Ljubljana Puppet Theatre and
Museum of Puppetry
Kaiu Meiner
Mladinska knjiga Publishing House
Daniel Muzyczuk
National Gallery of Slovenia
Nome Gallery
Natia Mikeladse-Bachsoliani and
Goethe-Zentrum, Yerevan
Ana Ofak
Hana Ostan Ožbolt
Berenika Partum
Nataša Petrešin-Bachelez
Irena Popiashvili
Salinen Prosol d.o.o.
Raster Gallery
Marijan Rupert and National and
University Library of Slovenia
Salon 94 Design
Sariev Contemporary
Aaron Schuster
Sergey Shabohin
Alenka Simončič
Society for Theoretical Psychoanalysis
Uroš Škerl
Tanya Bonakdar Gallery
Sarah Johanna Theurer and
Kraupa-Tuskany Zeidler
Vanda Vremšak Richter
Zavod Strip art

and the upcoming 2nd edition, 2020
Center for Contemporary Art
Ujazdowski Castle
Jazdów 2, 00-467
Warsaw, Poland

Director
Małgorzata Ludwisiak
Deputy Director
Urszula Kropiwiec
Artistic Director
Jarosław Lubiak
Assistant Curator
Michał Grzegorzek

The book was published as a part of
the 33rd Ljubljana Biennial of Graphic Arts
Crack Up – Crack Down

Published and distributed by
Mousse Publishing
Contrappunto s.r.l. Socio Unico
Corso di Porta Romana 63
20122, Milan, Italy

International Centre of Graphic Arts
(MGLC)
Grad Tivoli, Pod turnom 3
1000 Ljubljana, Slovenia

Available through
Mousse Publishing,
Milan
moussepublishing.com

DAP | Distributed Art Publishers,
New York
artbook.com

Vice Versa Distribution,
Berlin
viceversaartbooks.com

Les presses du réel,
Dijon
lespressesdureel.com

Antenne Books,
London
antennebooks.com

First edition: 1,200 copies, 2019

Printed on
Condat Matt Périgord 115 g/m²
Symbol Card 2 250 g/m²

Printed in Germany by
medialis Offsetdruck GmbH
Heidelberger Strasse 65/66
12435 Berlin, Germany

CIP - Kataložni zapis o publikaciji
Narodna in univerzitetna knjižnica, Ljubljana

76(100)"20"

GRAFIČNI bienale Ljubljana
(33 ; 2019 ; Ljubljana)
Crack up - crack down / 33rd Ljubljana Biennial of Graphic Arts ; [edited by] Slavs and Tatars, [M. Constantine] ; [Slovene-to-English translation Maja Lovrenov ; illustrations Nejc Prah]. - 1st ed. - Milan : Mousse Publishing ; Ljubljana : International Centre of Graphic Arts, 2019

ISBN 978-88-6749-388-3
(Mousse Publishing)
ISBN 978-961-6229-76-0
(International Centre of Graphic Arts)
1. Gl. stv. nasl.
COBISS.SI-ID 301552896

Price: €27 / $30

The publishers would like to thank all those who have kindly given their permission for the reproduction of material for this book. Every effort has been made to obtain permission to reproduce the images and texts in this catalogue. However, as is standard editorial policy, the publishers are at the disposal of copyright holders and undertake to correct any omissions or errors in future editions.

Cooperation and financial support

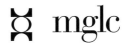

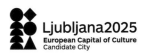

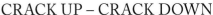

mglc

U–jazdowski

REPUBLIKA SLOVENIJA
MINISTRSTVO ZA KULTURO

Mestna občina
Ljubljana

LJUBLJANA
Zmagovalka 2016
ZELENA
PRESTOLNICA EVROPE

UNESCO
Organizacija Združenih narodov za izobraževanje, znanost in kulturo
LJUBLJANA: MESTO/CITY OF/LITERA-TURE ...
Unescovo kreativno mesto od 2015

Ljubljana2025
European Capital of Culture
Candidate City

Amanda Ross-Ho, ***Untitled Crisis Actor (HURTS WORST 2)***, 2019.

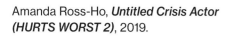

→
Hinko Smrekar, *Slovenian Art Exhibition*, ca. 1910. Courtesy of the National Gallery of Slovenia. *Translation of a text on the artwork by Hinko Smrekar: "Who knows, such an exhibition of Slovenian art might even be pleasing, after all?"